The Most Satisfying Strategies for Business Financing

John E. Cornish III

Copyright © 2023 John E. Cornish III

All rights reserved.

ISBN: **9781790345823**

The Most Satisfying Strategizing for Business Financing

FOREWORD

In today's fast-paced and ever-evolving business landscape, the ability to secure adequate financing is essential for success. Whether you are an aspiring entrepreneur launching a startup or a seasoned business owner seeking growth opportunities, understanding the intricacies of business financing is a vital skill.

I am delighted to introduce this comprehensive guide on strategies for business financing, tax incentives, and the benefits of having a trust. Within these pages, you will find a wealth of knowledge and practical advice to navigate the complex world of financing and unlock the power of financial resources to fuel your business's growth.

The authors have meticulously compiled a diverse range of topics, covering traditional financing options, alternative funding strategies, tax incentives, and the advantages of establishing a trust. They provide valuable insights into how businesses can optimize their financial positions, reduce tax burdens, and leverage various financing options to propel their ventures forward.

This book is not just a theoretical exploration of financing concepts; it is a practical roadmap that empowers entrepreneurs and business owners to take control of their financial destinies. The authors have drawn from their extensive expertise and experience to deliver actionable strategies, case studies, and best practices that you can implement in your own business.

One of the most significant strengths of this book is its comprehensive coverage. From understanding the fundamentals of business financing to exploring the nuances of tax incentives, trust structures, and financial management, you will gain a holistic understanding of the key components that contribute to a robust and sustainable financial foundation.

I urge you to approach this book as more than just a passive reader. Dive deep into each chapter, reflect on the strategies presented, and consider how they apply to your unique business circumstances. Take advantage of the case studies, practical tips, and expert insights to shape your financial strategies and embark on a path of sustainable growth.

Remember, knowledge is power, but it is action that leads to results. Use this book as a catalyst to propel your business forward, to seek new opportunities, and to embrace the financial strategies that align with your vision and goals.

I commend the authors for their dedication and expertise in crafting this invaluable resource. I have no doubt that it will serve as a guiding light for entrepreneurs and business owners as they navigate the complex terrain of business financing.

I wish you all the success in your journey towards unlocking the power of business financing and realizing the full potential of your ventures.

Contents

Chapter 1 14

Chapter 2 30

Chapter 3 48

Chapter 4 62

Chapter 5: 89

Chapter 6 97

Chapter 7 104

Chapter 8 110

Chapter 9 120

Chapter 10 126

Chapter 11 132

Chapter 12 138

Chapter 13 144

Chapter 14 150

Chapter 15 156

Chapter 16 164

Chapter 17 172

Chapter 18 179

Chapter 19 186

Chapter *20* 195

Chapter 21 201

The Most Satisfying Strategizing for Business Financing

The Most Satisfying Strategizing for Business Financing

The Most Satisfying Strategizing for Business Financing

PLUS 3 BONUS CHAPTERS

Indexing Note: This index is a general outline and may not include every subtopic covered in the book. The final index may vary based on the specific content included in the book.

Note: Each chapter will provide detailed information, practical tips, and real-world examples to help readers understand and implement the strategies discussed.

The book will be a comprehensive guide to business financing, with a focus on leveraging tax incentives and utilizing trusts to maximize financial benefits.

DISCLAIMER:

The information provided in this book is for educational and informational purposes only. It is not intended to be, nor should it be construed as, financial, or legal advice. The authors and publishers of this book are not financial advisors or legal professionals, and they do not assume any responsibility or liability for any actions taken based on the information provided in this book.

While the authors have made every effort to ensure the accuracy and completeness of the information presented, business and financial landscapes are subject to change,

and laws and regulations may vary across jurisdictions. It is essential to consult with qualified financial advisors, tax professionals, and legal experts before making any financial decisions or implementing any strategies discussed in this book.

Every business is unique, and the suitability and applicability of any financing strategy or tax incentive may vary based on individual circumstances. The readers are encouraged to conduct their own research, perform due diligence, and seek professional advice tailored to their specific needs and goals.

The authors and publishers disclaim any liability for the outcomes or consequences of any actions taken based on the information provided in this book. The readers bear sole responsibility for their financial decisions, and they should exercise caution and prudence when implementing any financial strategies or engaging in any financial activities.

It is important to recognize that business financing involves risks, and past success stories or case studies mentioned in this book do not guarantee similar outcomes in the future. The results achieved by other businesses are dependent on numerous factors that may not be replicable or applicable to every situation.

By reading this book, you acknowledge and agree that the authors and publishers shall not be held liable for any damages, losses, or liabilities arising directly or indirectly from the use or application of the information presented herein.

Always consult with qualified professionals and trusted advisors who are familiar with your specific circumstances before making any financial decisions. Your own research, analysis, and judgment should be used in evaluating the information provided in this book, and you should exercise caution and seek professional guidance where appropriate.

Chapter 1

Understanding Business Financing:

Business financing refers to the methods, strategies, and processes involved in securing capital to support the operations, growth, and expansion of a business. It encompasses the financial resources and mechanisms used to acquire assets, invest in projects, manage cash flow, and meet financial obligations.

Importance of Understanding Business Financing:

Sound financial management and adequate financing are crucial for the success of any business. It enables businesses to seize opportunities, navigate challenges, and

achieve their growth objectives. Understanding business financing helps entrepreneurs and business owners make informed decisions about the most suitable financing options for their specific needs and circumstances. It allows businesses to optimize their capital structure, balance risk and return, and ensure sustainable financial health.

Financing Options:

Debt Financing: Debt financing involves borrowing money from lenders, such as banks or financial institutions, with the obligation to repay the principal amount along with interest over a specified period. It can take various forms, including bank loans, lines of credit, and equipment financing.

Equity Financing:

Equity financing involves raising capital by selling ownership stakes in the business.

Investors, such as venture capitalists or angel investors, provide funding in exchange for equity ownership or shares in the business.

Alternative Financing:

Alternative financing methods have gained popularity in recent years. These include crowdfunding, peer to peer lending, revenue-based financing, and invoice financing. These methods offer alternative sources of capital outside of traditional banking or investment channels.

Assessing Financing Needs:

Before seeking financing, businesses need to assess their financial needs accurately. This involves evaluating the purpose of financing, such as funding expansion, launching a new product, or managing cash flow.

Businesses should conduct a comprehensive financial analysis, including cash flow projections, budgeting, and assessing their working capital requirements. This evaluation helps determine the amount of capital needed and the appropriate financing options.

Financial Statements and Documentation:

Lenders and investors typically require financial statements and documentation to assess the creditworthiness and financial health of a business. Key financial statements include the balance sheet, income statement, and cash flow statement. These statements provide insights into the business's assets, liabilities, revenues, expenses, and cash flow patterns.

Businesses should maintain accurate and up-to-date financial records, as they play a crucial role in securing financing.

Building a Strong Financing Plan:

Developing a financing plan is essential for articulating the business's financing needs, identifying the most suitable financing options, and creating a roadmap for securing capital. The financing plan should outline the purpose of the financing, the amount needed, the expected return on investment, and the proposed repayment terms. It should also include a comprehensive business plan, market analysis, and financial projections to demonstrate the viability and potential for success.

Securing Financing:

Once the financing plan is in place, businesses can begin the process of securing financing. This involves identifying potential lenders or investors, preparing loan applications or investment pitches, and engaging in negotiations. Effective communication and a compelling pitch that highlights the business's value proposition, growth potential, and financial stability are essential in securing financing.

Managing Post-Funding Relationships:

After securing financing, businesses must effectively manage their relationships with lenders or investors. This includes fulfilling repayment obligations, providing regular financial updates and maintaining transparency.

Building strong relationships with financiers can provide additional support, access to future funding, and potential strategic partnerships. Understanding business financing is crucial for businesses to make informed decisions about their financial needs, evaluate financing options, and secure the necessary capital to support their growth and success. By developing a comprehensive understanding of business financing, entrepreneurs and business owners can navigate the complexities of the financial landscape, optimize their financial strategies, and position their businesses for long-term prosperity.

Financial Analysis and Forecasting:

Understanding business financing also requires proficiency in financial analysis and forecasting. This involves assessing the financial health of the business, analyzing key financial ratios, and projecting future financial performance. Financial analysis helps identify strengths and weaknesses in the business's financial position, allowing for informed decision-making regarding financing options. Forecasting future financial performance enables businesses to anticipate funding requirements, plan for contingencies, and make strategic financial decisions.

Risk Assessment and Mitigation:

Business financing is inherently associated with risks. Understanding these risks and implementing strategies to mitigate them is essential for sustainable financial management. Risk assessment involves identifying potential risks, such as market volatility, economic downturns, or changes in regulatory environments, that may impact the business's financial stability and ability to repay debts.

Mitigation strategies may include diversifying sources of financing, maintaining a healthy cash reserve, obtaining appropriate insurance coverage, and implementing risk management practices.

Cash Flow Management:

Effective cash flow management is a critical aspect of business financing. It involves monitoring cash inflows and outflows, ensuring sufficient liquidity to meet financial obligations, and optimizing working capital.

Understanding cash flow patterns, including revenue cycles, payment terms, and operating expenses, helps businesses plan for funding needs, negotiate favorable payment terms, and make timely decisions regarding capital investments.

Financial Efficiency and Optimization:

Understanding business financing extends beyond securing capital. It also involves optimizing financial efficiency to maximize profitability and return on investment.

This may include implementing cost control measures, improving operational efficiency,

negotiating favorable terms with suppliers and optimizing pricing strategies. By enhancing financial efficiency, businesses can generate higher profits, reduce reliance on external financing, and improve their overall financial position.

Monitoring and Adjusting Financing Strategies:

Business financing is not a one-time event but an ongoing process. It requires continuous monitoring and evaluation of the financing strategies implemented.

Regularly reviewing the effectiveness of financing methods, assessing changes in the business's financial needs, and adjusting financing strategies accordingly is crucial for long-term success. Monitoring the impact of financing decisions on the business's financial performance, profitability, and cash flow enables businesses to make informed adjustments and optimize their financing approach.

Staying Informed and Adapting to Market Trends:

The business financing landscape is dynamic, influenced by market trends, economic conditions, and regulatory changes. Understanding business financing necessitates staying informed and adapting to these market dynamics.

Keeping abreast of financial news, industry trends, and changes in regulatory policies helps businesses identify new financing opportunities, anticipate potential challenges, and adapt their strategies accordingly.

Actively participating in industry networks,

attending relevant conferences and seminars, and engaging with professional associations can provide valuable insights and networking opportunities to stay informed about emerging financing practices. By thoroughly understanding business financing, entrepreneurs, and business owners can effectively navigate financial complexities, make informed decisions, and position their businesses for sustainable growth and success. It enables them to optimize their financial strategies, mitigate risks, and adapt to evolving market conditions, ultimately enhancing their competitiveness in the business landscape.

Collaboration with Financial Professionals:

While understanding business financing is crucial, it is also important to recognize the value of collaborating with financial professionals. Engaging the expertise of accountants, financial advisors, and business consultants can provide valuable insights, guidance, and support.

Financial professionals have in-depth knowledge of the intricacies of business financing, tax incentives, and trust structures. They can assist in assessing financing needs, developing comprehensive financing plans, and identifying appropriate financing options. These professionals can also provide valuable advice on tax optimization strategies, including leveraging tax incentives and structuring trusts effectively to maximize financial benefits. Collaborating with financial professionals fosters a collaborative approach to financial management and ensures businesses have access to the latest industry insights and best practices.

Continuous Learning and Adaptation:

Understanding business financing is not a one-time achievement but an ongoing process. The financial landscape is dynamic and constantly evolving, requiring continuous learning and adaptation.

Business owners and entrepreneurs should actively seek opportunities to expand their knowledge and stay updated on new financing options, tax incentives, and regulatory changes. Participating in professional development programs, attending workshops or seminars, and engaging in industry forums can provide valuable learning experiences and help businesses stay ahead of the curve. Additionally, fostering a mindset of continuous improvement and adaptability enables businesses to adjust their financing strategies in response to changing market conditions and emerging opportunities.

Case Studies and Real-World Examples:

To enhance understanding of business financing strategies, this book will include case studies and real-world examples throughout the chapters. These case studies will highlight how different businesses have successfully navigated financing challenges, utilized tax incentives, and implemented trust structures to achieve their financial objectives.

Analyzing real-life scenarios and learning from practical examples can provide valuable insights and inspire innovative approaches to business financing.

Self-Assessment and Reflection:

Understanding business financing requires self-assessment and reflection on the unique needs and circumstances of each business. Throughout the book, readers will be encouraged to engage in self-assessment exercises and reflection activities to evaluate their current financial position, identify areas for improvement, and align their financing strategies with their specific business goals.

By engaging in self-assessment and reflection, readers can customize the strategies presented in the book to suit their individual business needs and foster a deeper understanding of their financial requirements.

Conclusion:

Understanding business financing is a fundamental aspect of successful financial management. It involves comprehending various financing options, assessing financial needs, analyzing risks, optimizing financial efficiency, and staying informed about market trends.

Collaborating with financial professionals, continuous learning, and engaging in self-assessment activities are crucial for building a strong foundation in business financing. By developing a deep understanding of business financing, entrepreneurs and business owners can make informed decisions, secure the necessary capital, and effectively manage their financial resources to achieve their long-term goals. The chapter on understanding business financing emphasizes the importance of collaboration with financial professionals, continuous learning, and self-assessment. It also highlights the value of real-world examples, case studies, and the need for adaptation in the dynamic financial landscape. By comprehending the principles and strategies of business financing, readers can lay a solid foundation for their financial success.

Chapter 2

Leveraging Tax Incentives for Business Financing:

Tax incentives are government-initiated measures designed to encourage certain behaviors or stimulate economic growth. They can provide significant financial benefits for businesses, including reducing tax liabilities, promoting investment, and supporting business expansion. Understanding and effectively leveraging tax incentives is a crucial aspect of business financing. Here are key points to consider:

Types of Tax Incentives:

Tax incentives can take various forms, including tax credits, deductions, exemptions, and deferrals. Each type of incentive is designed to incentivize specific activities or investments.

Examples of tax incentives include research and development (R&D) tax credits, investment tax credits, accelerated depreciation, energy-efficient tax incentives, and job creation incentives. It is important for businesses to identify and understand the tax incentives available to them based on their industry, location, and activities.

Benefits of Tax Incentives:

Tax incentives provide direct financial benefits to businesses by reducing their tax burden. This allows businesses to allocate more funds toward operational expenses, investment, and growth initiatives. By leveraging tax incentives, businesses can increase their cash flow, enhance profitability, and gain a competitive advantage.

Additionally, tax incentives can encourage businesses to engage in activities that benefit the broader economy, such as research and development, job creation, and investment in sustainable practices.

Research and Identification:

Businesses need to conduct thorough research to identify and understand the tax incentives available to them. This involves consulting tax professionals, reviewing government websites, and engaging with industry associations to stay informed about the latest incentives and eligibility criteria. It is important to note that tax incentives can vary by jurisdiction, industry, and business size. Therefore, businesses should ensure they meet the specific requirements to qualify for the incentives.

Strategic Tax Planning:

Leveraging tax incentives effectively requires strategic tax planning. Businesses should align their activities and investments with incentives to optimize their tax benefits.

This may involve timing expenditures to coincide with eligibility periods, structuring investments to maximize tax credits, or identifying eligible expenses for deductions.

Businesses should work closely with tax professionals to develop a comprehensive tax planning strategy that takes advantage of available incentives while remaining compliant with tax laws and regulations.

Compliance and Documentation:

To benefit from tax incentives, businesses must comply with the reporting and documentation requirements associated with each incentive.

It is essential to maintain accurate and detailed records of eligible expenses, investments, and activities related to the incentives. Documentation should include invoices, receipts, contracts, employment records, and

other supporting documents necessary to substantiate claims for the incentives.

Regular Review and Update:

Tax incentives are subject to change as governments modify their policies and priorities. It is crucial for businesses to regularly review and update their knowledge of available incentives.

Staying informed about changes in tax laws and regulations, as well as new incentives introduced, ensures businesses do not miss out on potential opportunities for financial benefits.

Collaboration with Tax Professionals:

Collaborating with tax professionals, such as accountants or tax advisors, is highly recommended when leveraging tax incentives.

Tax professionals have the expertise to navigate the complexities of tax laws, interpret eligibility requirements, and maximize the benefits for businesses.

They can provide guidance on tax planning strategies, assist with documentation, and ensure compliance with tax regulations.

Integration with Overall Financial Strategy:

Leveraging tax incentives should be integrated into the overall financial strategy of the business. Businesses should consider the impact of tax incentives on their cash flow, profitability, and long-term financial goals.

By aligning tax incentives with the broader financial objectives of the business, businesses can optimize their financial performance and achieve sustainable growth.

Continuous Monitoring and Adjustment:

Tax incentives may have expiration dates or changing eligibility criteria. It is essential for businesses to continuously monitor changes in tax laws and regulations to ensure ongoing compliance and eligibility.

Regularly reviewing the effectiveness of tax planning strategies and adjusting them as needed allows businesses to maximize their tax benefits and adapt to evolving incentive programs.

Professional Development and Training:

Developing an understanding of tax incentives requires continuous professional development and training. Businesses should invest in educating their finance and accounting teams to stay up to date with changes in tax laws and regulations, as well as the latest developments in tax incentives. This ensures that businesses can proactively identify opportunities, optimize their tax planning strategies, and effectively leverage available incentives.

Leveraging tax incentives for business financing can significantly enhance a business's financial position and support its growth. By staying informed, strategically planning, collaborating with tax professionals, and integrating tax incentives into the overall financial strategy, businesses can optimize their tax benefits and achieve their financial objectives. However, it is important to ensure compliance with tax laws and regulations to avoid any penalties or legal issues.

Examples of Tax Incentives:

Research and Development (R&D) Tax Credits: Many governments offer tax credits to businesses that invest in research and development activities. These credits provide financial incentives to encourage innovation and technological advancement.

Investment Tax Credits:

Governments may provide tax credits to businesses that invest in certain sectors or industries, such as renewable energy, infrastructure development, or job creation initiatives. These credits can offset a portion of the investment costs.

Accelerated Depreciation:

Some tax systems allow for accelerated

depreciation of assets, allowing businesses to deduct a larger portion of the asset's cost in the early years of its useful life. This can provide significant tax savings and improve cash flow.

Energy-Efficient Tax Incentives:

Governments may offer tax incentives to businesses that implement energy-efficient practices, invest in renewable energy systems, or use energy-efficient equipment. These incentives aim to promote sustainable business practices and reduce environmental impact.

Job Creation Incentives:

To stimulate employment, governments may provide tax incentives to businesses that create new jobs or hire individuals from specific target groups, such as veterans, long-term unemployed individuals, or individuals from disadvantaged communities.

Export Incentives:

Governments may offer tax incentives to businesses that engage in export activities, such as tax credits or exemptions on export-related income or favorable tax treatment for export-oriented businesses.

Regional Development Incentives:

Governments often provide tax incentives to businesses that operate in poor regions. These incentives can include tax credits, exemptions, or reduced tax rates to encourage investment and job creation in these areas.

Benefits of Leveraging Tax Incentives for Business Financing, Reduced Tax Liability:

The primary benefit of leveraging tax incentives is the reduction of tax liabilities, allowing businesses to retain more of their earnings and allocate funds towards growth initiatives or operational expenses.

Increased Cash Flow:

Tax incentives can enhance cash flow by providing immediate or deferred tax benefits. This additional liquidity enables businesses to invest in expansion, research and development, or other strategic initiatives.

Competitive Advantage:

Utilizing tax incentives effectively can give businesses a competitive edge by lowering costs and enhancing profitability. It allows businesses to invest in areas that enhance their competitiveness, such as technology upgrades, employee training, or product innovation.

Encouraging Investment and Growth:

Tax incentives are designed to stimulate investment and economic growth. By leveraging these incentives, businesses are encouraged to expand their operations, invest in new technologies, create jobs, and contribute to overall economic development.

Improved Financial Position:

By optimizing tax incentives, businesses can improve their financial position, strengthen their balance sheets, and enhance their ability to secure additional financing or attract investment.

Positive Public Image:

Leveraging tax incentives to support socially responsible activities, such as environmental sustainability or job creation, can enhance a business's reputation and public image. This can lead to increased customer loyalty, brand value, and market opportunities.

Key Considerations and Challenges:

Eligibility Criteria: Each tax incentive program has specific eligibility criteria that businesses must meet to qualify. It is important to thoroughly understand these criteria and ensure compliance to fully benefit from the incentives.

Documentation and Reporting:

Proper documentation and reporting are crucial when claiming tax incentives. Businesses should maintain accurate records of eligible activities, expenses, and investments to substantiate their claims.

Changing Regulations:

Tax laws and regulations are subject to change, and governments may modify or discontinue tax incentives over time. Businesses must stay updated on the latest changes to ensure continued eligibility and compliance.

Balancing Multiple Incentives:

Businesses operating in multiple jurisdictions may have access to different tax incentives. It can be challenging to navigate and optimize the benefits of multiple incentives while managing compliance requirements.

Consultation with Tax Professionals:

Due to the complexity of tax laws and

incentives, consulting with tax professionals is highly recommended. They can provide guidance, ensure compliance, and help businesses optimize their tax planning strategies. Leveraging tax incentives for business financing can be a powerful tool for businesses to reduce tax liabilities, improve cash flow, gain a competitive advantage, and stimulate growth. However, it requires careful planning, ongoing compliance, and a thorough understanding of the available incentives. By strategically incorporating tax incentives into their financial strategies, businesses can unlock significant financial benefits and enhance their overall financial position.

Case Studies:

To further illustrate the practical application of leveraging tax incentives for business financing, let's examine a couple of case studies:

Case Study 1: Green Energy Company

A renewable energy company specializing in solar power installation and maintenance wanted to expand its operations and invest in new equipment. By leveraging tax incentives, they were able to achieve their financing goals while reducing their tax liability.

First, the company researched and identified the available tax incentives for renewable energy businesses. They discovered a combination of investment tax credits and accelerated depreciation options. These incentives allowed them to offset a significant portion of their investment costs and reduce their tax burden.

Next, the company strategically planned its investment and equipment purchases to align with the eligibility periods of the incentives. By carefully timing their expenditures, they maximized the tax benefits. The company collaborated with tax professionals who helped them navigate the complex requirements of the incentives. They ensured proper documentation and compliance with reporting obligations to substantiate their claims. As a result, the company successfully expanded its operations, acquired state-of-the-art equipment, and significantly reduced its tax liabilities. The tax incentives not only improved their cash flow but also enhanced their competitive position in the renewable energy market.

Case Study 2: Research and Development (R&D) Tax Credits

A technology startup engaged in software development aimed to enhance its research and development efforts. By leveraging R&D tax credits, they were able to access additional funds for their innovation initiatives. The startup conducted thorough research to understand the eligibility criteria and requirements for R&D tax credits. They collaborated with tax professionals who helped them identify eligible R&D activities and expenses.

The company developed a comprehensive tax planning strategy that focused on maximizing their R&D tax credits. They ensured that their documentation accurately captured their R&D efforts, including project plans, employee records, and expense reports.

By effectively leveraging the R&D tax credits, the startup was able to offset a significant portion of their R&D costs. This allowed them to invest more in research and innovation, hire additional talent, and accelerate product development. These case studies highlight the importance of researching available tax incentives, strategically planning investments, collaborating with tax professionals, and maintaining accurate documentation. By leveraging tax incentives effectively, businesses can achieve their financing objectives, enhance their competitiveness, and stimulate growth and innovation.

Conclusion:

Leveraging tax incentives for business financing can provide substantial financial benefits and support business growth. By understanding the different types of incentives, conducting thorough research, strategic tax planning, and collaborating with tax professionals, businesses can optimize their tax benefits and improve their financial position.

It is crucial for businesses to stay updated on changes in tax laws and regulations, as well as evolving incentive programs. Regular review, monitoring, and adjustment of tax planning strategies are essential to ensure continued eligibility and compliance.

Ultimately, by effectively leveraging tax incentives, businesses can reduce tax liabilities, enhance cash flow, gain a competitive advantage, stimulate investment, and contribute to their overall financial success.

Chapter 3

The Benefits of Trust for Business Financing:

In addition to tax incentives, another valuable strategy for business financing is the utilization of trusts. A trust is a legal entity that allows the transfer of assets to a trustee who manages and distributes those assets according to specific instructions outlined in the trust document. Here are some key benefits of incorporating trusts into business financing:

Asset Protection:

One significant advantage of utilizing a trust is the protection it offers to business assets. By transferring assets to a trust, they are held separately from the business itself, which helps shield them from potential liabilities, lawsuits, or creditors. Trusts can provide a layer of protection against business risks, ensuring that assets are safeguarded even in the event of unforeseen circumstances or legal challenges.

Estate Planning and Succession:

Trusts play a crucial role in estate planning and business succession. By establishing a trust, business owners can determine how their assets will be distributed, ensuring a smooth transition of ownership in the future.

Trusts allow for flexibility in specifying beneficiaries, defining distribution plans, and setting conditions for asset transfer. This helps minimize family conflicts, maintain continuity in business operations and provide for the financial well-being of loved ones.

Privacy and Confidentiality:

Trusts offer a level of privacy and confidentiality that is not typically afforded by other business structures. Unlike publicly traded companies or partnerships, trust documents are private and not subject to public disclosure.

This can be particularly advantageous for businesses that value confidentiality, as trust ownership can help protect sensitive information, trade secrets, and proprietary business strategies from public scrutiny.

Tax Planning and Optimization:

Trusts can be effective tools for tax planning and optimization. Depending on the jurisdiction and specific trust structure, certain tax advantages may be available, such as reduced estate taxes or tax deferral on income generated by trust assets. By strategically organizing business assets within a trust, businesses can potentially minimize their tax liabilities and maximize their overall financial position.

Continuity and Business Stability:

Trusts can provide a mechanism for ensuring business continuity and stability, especially in situations where the owner or key stakeholders are unable to actively manage the business. By appointing a trustee and outlining clear instructions in the trust document, businesses can ensure that operations continue smoothly, key decisions are made in line with their vision, and long-term business goals are achieved.

Flexibility in Investment and Financing:

Trusts offer flexibility in investment and financing strategies. Trust assets can be used to secure loans or investments, providing additional avenues for capital acquisition and business expansion. Trusts can also facilitate collaboration with financial institutions, as the separation of assets within a trust can provide added security and collateral options for lenders.

Wealth Preservation and Charitable Giving:

Trusts can be used for wealth preservation and charitable giving purposes. Through charitable trusts, businesses can allocate a portion of their assets or income to charitable causes, creating a positive social impact while potentially receiving tax benefits. Trusts can also enable the preservation and management of wealth across generations, allowing businesses to support their beneficiaries and philanthropic endeavors in a structured and controlled manner. It is important to note that establishing a trust requires careful consideration and expert legal advice to ensure compliance with relevant laws and regulations. Businesses should consult with experienced professionals specializing in trust law to tailor trust structures to their specific needs and objectives.

By leveraging trusts as part of their business financing strategies, businesses can benefit from asset protection, estate planning, privacy, tax optimization, continuity, flexibility in investment, and philanthropic opportunities. Trusts provide a powerful framework for managing and preserving business assets, ensuring long-term financial security and stability.

Succession Planning and Business Continuity:

Trusts are valuable tools for succession planning, especially in family-owned businesses. By transferring ownership of business assets to a trust, business owners can ensure a smooth transition of control and management to the next generation. The trust document can outline specific instructions regarding the transfer of assets, the roles and responsibilities of beneficiaries, and the preservation of the business's mission and values. Trusts provide a structured framework for managing the transfer of ownership, minimizing potential conflicts or disputes, and maintaining the continuity of the business.

Creditor Protection:

Trusts can provide a level of protection against potential creditors. By transferring assets to a trust, those assets are no longer considered personal property and are separate from the business owner's individual liabilities.

This can be particularly advantageous in industries or situations where the risk of litigation or financial claims is high. Trusts can help safeguard business assets, ensuring that they remain protected even if the business owner faces personal financial challenges.

Estate Tax Planning:

Trusts are commonly used for estate tax planning purposes. Depending on the jurisdiction, trusts can offer tax advantages by reducing the taxable value of the estate or providing exemptions or deductions. By transferring assets to a trust, businesses can potentially minimize estate taxes, allowing more of the business's value to be passed on to beneficiaries or future generations.

Trusts can also provide greater control over the distribution of assets, ensuring that they are allocated according to the business owner's wishes and in a tax-efficient manner.

Investment Opportunities:

Trusts can open diverse investment opportunities for businesses. By transferring assets to a trust, businesses can expand their investment portfolio and diversify their holdings. Trusts can hold various types of assets, such as real estate, stocks, bonds, and other investment instruments. This enables businesses to take advantage of different investment strategies and potentially achieve higher returns.

Business Flexibility:

Trusts offer flexibility in adapting to changing business circumstances. The terms of the trust can be structured to allow for modifications, adjustments, or the addition of new assets.

This flexibility allows businesses to respond to market conditions, strategic opportunities, or shifts in their financial goals without the need for complex legal processes or restructuring.

Professional Management:

Trusts provide the option to appoint professional trustees or fiduciaries to manage the assets and operations of the trust. This can be particularly beneficial for businesses that require specialized expertise or professional management, allowing the business owner to focus on other aspects of their business or personal life while ensuring effective management of trust assets. By leveraging trusts for business financing, businesses can benefit from succession planning, creditor protection, estate tax planning, investment opportunities, flexibility, and professional management. Trusts provide a robust framework for managing business assets, protecting wealth, and ensuring the long-term success and sustainability of the business. However, it is crucial to work with experienced professionals specializing in trust law and consult with financial advisors to determine the most suitable trust structure and ensure compliance with applicable laws and regulations.

Risk Mitigation:

Trusts can serve as a risk mitigation tool for businesses. By transferring assets to a trust, businesses can separate their personal and business assets, minimizing the impact of potential business risks on their personal wealth. In the event of bankruptcy, lawsuits, or other financial challenges faced by the business, trust assets can be protected from seizure or liquidation, providing a layer of security for the business owner.

Confidentiality and Privacy:

Trusts offer a level of confidentiality and privacy that can be advantageous for businesses. Unlike other business entities that require public filings and disclosures, trust documents are typically not subject to public scrutiny.

This can be particularly important for businesses that value their competitive advantage, proprietary information, or wish to maintain a low profile in the public domain.

Enhanced Business Image and Professionalism:

Utilizing a trust structure can enhance the business's image and professionalism, particularly for high-net-worth individuals or family-owned businesses.

Trusts convey a sense of stability, organization, and long-term planning, which can inspire confidence in stakeholders, investors, and clients.

Charitable Giving and Philanthropy:

Trusts can facilitate charitable giving and philanthropic endeavors for businesses. By establishing charitable trusts, businesses can set aside assets or income specifically for charitable purposes. This allows businesses to contribute to causes they are passionate about, create a positive social impact, and potentially receive tax benefits for their charitable contributions.

Business Flexibility and Adaptability:

Trusts provide businesses with flexibility and adaptability in managing their assets. The terms of the trust can be customized to accommodate changing business needs, expansions, acquisitions, or diversification strategies.

This flexibility allows businesses to seize new opportunities, respond to market dynamics, and adjust their asset allocation as needed.

Multi-Generational Wealth Management:

Trusts are particularly valuable for multi-generational wealth management. By establishing trusts, businesses can ensure the preservation and smooth transfer of wealth across generations. Trusts provide a structured framework for managing assets, specifying beneficiaries, and outlining distribution plans, minimizing the potential for disputes or mismanagement of wealth.

Strategic Business Planning:

Trusts can play a role in strategic business planning by providing a long-term perspective and facilitating asset management aligned with business goals. Businesses can use trusts to set aside assets for specific purposes, such as future acquisitions, research and development initiatives, or expansion into new markets.

In conclusion, utilizing trusts for business financing can provide numerous benefits, including asset protection, estate planning, privacy, tax optimization, business continuity, investment flexibility, and philanthropic opportunities. Trusts offer businesses a powerful tool for managing assets, mitigating risks, and planning for the long-term success and sustainability of the business. It is essential to work with experienced legal and financial professionals to design and implement trusts tailored to the specific needs and objectives of the business.

Chapter 4

Creating and Managing a Trust:

Creating and managing a trust requires careful consideration and expert guidance to ensure its effectiveness and compliance with relevant laws and regulations. Here are the key steps involved in creating and managing a trust for business purposes:

Determine the Purpose and Goals:

Clearly define the purpose and goals of the trust. Identify why you want to create a trust for your business, whether it's for asset protection, estate planning, tax optimization, or other specific objectives. Consider the long-term vision for your business and how trust can support that vision. This will help shape the trust's structure and provisions.

Seek Professional Advice:

Consult with experienced professionals specializing in trust law, such as attorneys and financial advisors. They will provide valuable insights, ensure compliance with legal requirements, and guide you through the trust creation process. Work with professionals who have expertise in both trust law and business law to ensure that the trust aligns with your business objectives.

Choose the Right Trust Structure:

Select the appropriate trust structure that suits your business needs. Common types of trusts include revocable trusts, irrevocable trusts, living trusts, family trusts, and charitable trusts. Each trust structure has its own advantages, limitations, and tax implications. Your

professional advisors can help you determine the most suitable structure based on your specific goals and circumstances.

Identify the Trustee:

Select a trustee to manage the trust and its assets. The trustee can be an individual, a professional trustee, or a corporate trustee. Consider factors such as trustworthiness, financial acumen, and knowledge of your business when choosing a trustee. The trustee should act in the best interests of the trust and its beneficiaries.

Draft the Trust Agreement:

Work with your attorney to draft the trust agreement, which is the legal document that outlines the terms and conditions of the trust. The trust agreement should clearly define the purpose of the trust, identify the trustee and beneficiaries, specify the assets to be transferred to the trust, and detail the powers and responsibilities of the trustee. Include provisions that address contingencies, such as the removal or replacement of the trustee, changes in beneficiaries, and dispute resolution mechanisms.

Fund the Trust:

Transfer the business assets into the trust according to the terms outlined in the trust agreement. This typically involves changing the ownership of the assets from the business owner to the trust. It is important to follow proper legal and accounting procedures to ensure the valid transfer of assets to the trust.

Trust Administration:

Once the trust is established and funded, ongoing trust administration is necessary. The trustee is responsible for managing the trust assets, making distributions, and ensuring compliance with legal and tax requirements.

Regular communication between the trustee and the business owner is crucial to keep track of the trust's performance, address any changes in business circumstances, and evaluate the need for adjustments to the trust provisions.

Periodic Review and Updates:

Periodically review the trust provisions to ensure they remain aligned with your business goals and any changes in laws or regulations. Change in business circumstances, ownership structure, or tax laws may require updates to the trust agreement. Consult with your legal and financial advisors to determine if any modifications are necessary.

Recordkeeping and Reporting:

Maintain accurate records of trust transactions, income, expenses, and distributions. This includes proper accounting and bookkeeping for the trust's financial activities. Comply with reporting obligations, such as filing tax returns for the trust and providing necessary documentation to beneficiaries.

Regular Communication and Review:

Maintain open communication with the trustee and beneficiaries of the trust. Provide updates on the business's performance, significant changes in operations, and any relevant information regarding the trust assets or distributions. Regularly review the trust's performance and consult with your professional advisors to assess if the trust is still meeting its intended goals and objectives.

Discuss any changes in business circumstances, financial goals, or succession plans with the trustee to ensure the trust remains aligned with your evolving business needs.

Compliance with Legal and Tax Requirements:

Ensure ongoing compliance with legal and tax requirements related to the trust. This includes staying informed about any changes in trust laws and regulations that may impact the trust's administration or tax implications.

Work closely with your legal and financial advisors to understand and fulfill any reporting obligations, tax filings, or other legal requirements associated with the trust.

Succession Planning and Review:

Incorporate trust into your overall business succession plan. Regularly review and update the trust provisions to reflect changes in your succession plan and ensure a smooth transition of ownership and management.

Consider how trust can support the long-term sustainability and continuity of the business beyond your involvement.

Monitor Trust Performance:

Regularly monitor the performance of the trust's assets. Evaluate the investment strategies, assess the risk profile, and adjust if necessary to optimize the trust's performance.

Maintain a clear understanding of the trust's financial position, including income, expenses, and growth, to ensure that the trust is contributing to your business's financial goals.

Periodic Trust Reviews:

Conduct periodic reviews of the trust structure and provisions to determine if any changes or updates are necessary. This includes considering changes in tax laws, business objectives, or family dynamics that may impact the trust's effectiveness. Engage with your professional advisors to assess the ongoing relevance and suitability of the trust for your business needs.

Communication with Beneficiaries:

Maintain open and transparent communication with the trust beneficiaries. Provide regular updates on the trust's performance, changes in trust provisions, and any significant decisions that may affect them. Foster a clear understanding of the purpose and benefits of the trust to ensure a harmonious relationship with the beneficiaries.

Remember, creating and managing a trust for business purposes is a complex and highly specialized area. It is crucial to work closely with qualified professionals, such as attorneys, accountants, and financial advisors, who have expertise in trust law and business planning. They will guide you through the process, help you navigate legal and tax complexities, and ensure that the trust is structured and managed effectively to support your business financing goals.

Review and Adjust Trust Provisions:

Regularly review the trust provisions to ensure they align with your evolving business needs and objectives. Changes in business structure, ownership, or goals may require modifications to the trust.

Work with your legal and financial advisors to assess the effectiveness of the trust provisions and make any necessary adjustments to optimize its benefits for your business.

Monitor Legal and Regulatory Changes:

Stay informed about changes in trust laws, tax

regulations, and other relevant legal requirements. Changes in legislation can impact the administration and taxation of trusts. Regularly consult with your legal and financial advisors to ensure ongoing compliance with applicable laws and take advantage of any new opportunities or incentives.

Conduct Periodic Trust Reviews:

Conduct regular reviews of the trust's performance and effectiveness. Assess whether the trust is achieving its intended goals and providing the desired benefits for your business. Evaluate the trust's asset allocation, investment performance, and overall management. Consider whether any adjustments are necessary to align the trust with your changing business circumstances.

Educate and Involve Trustees and Beneficiaries:

Educate the trustees and beneficiaries about the trust's purpose, provisions, and long-term objectives. Ensure they understand their roles and responsibilities.

Foster open communication and regular updates to keep all parties informed about the trust's performance, changes in strategy, and any decisions that may impact them.

Seek Ongoing Professional Guidance:

Continuously work with experienced professionals who specialize in trust management and business financing. They can provide valuable insights, monitor the trust's performance, and offer guidance on maximizing its benefits. Regularly consult with your legal, financial, and tax advisors to address any concerns, explore new opportunities, and ensure that the trust remains aligned with your business financing strategy.

Maintain Accurate Recordkeeping:

Maintain accurate and organized records of all trust-related transactions, including asset transfers, income, expenses, and distributions. Proper recordkeeping is crucial for compliance, reporting, and transparency. Follow best practices in accounting and recordkeeping to ensure that the trust's financial activities are well-documented and easily accessible for review.

Review Succession Planning:

Incorporate the trust into your overall business succession plan. Regularly review and update the succession plan to ensure that the trust's provisions align with your desired outcomes for the future of your business.

Consider changes in the leadership team, family dynamics, or business goals that may require adjustments to the trust provisions or succession plan.

Continual Monitoring of Business and Market Conditions:

Continually monitor the business and market

conditions to assess the ongoing relevance and effectiveness of the trust. External factors such as changes in the industry, economic conditions, or legal landscape may necessitate adjustments to the trust strategy.

Regular Communication and Collaboration:

Foster regular communication and collaboration among all parties involved in the trust. This includes the business owner, trustees, beneficiaries, and professional advisors.

Encourage open dialogue to address any concerns, share updates, and ensure that everyone is aligned with the trust's objectives and strategies.

By following these steps and maintaining ongoing management and review processes, you can effectively create and manage a trust for your business financing needs. The involvement of knowledgeable professionals and regular assessments will help ensure that the trust remains a valuable tool in supporting your business's financial goals and long-term success.

Regular Trustee Meetings:

Schedule regular trustee meetings to discuss the trust's performance, investment strategy, and any significant decisions or changes. These meetings provide an opportunity for trustees to collaborate, review financial reports and make informed decisions. Trustee meetings also allow for the exchange of ideas, clarification of roles and responsibilities, and the identification of any emerging issues that need attention.

Review and Update Beneficiary Designations:

Periodically review and update beneficiary designations to reflect any changes in your business structure, family circumstances, or estate planning goals.

Consider the needs and preferences of your beneficiaries and ensure that their interests are appropriately addressed in the trust provisions.

Regular Reporting to Beneficiaries:

Provide regular reports to the beneficiaries, outlining the trust's financial performance, distributions, and any other relevant information. Transparency and clear communication help build trust and maintain a positive relationship with beneficiaries, fostering a sense of confidence and understanding of the trust's activities.

Tax Planning and Compliance:

Work closely with your tax advisor to develop effective tax planning strategies that maximize the benefits of the trust structure for your business.

Stay updated on tax laws and regulations to ensure ongoing compliance with reporting requirements, tax filings, and any potential tax incentives or deductions available to the trust.

Risk Management:

Implement robust risk management practices to protect the trust assets and minimize potential risks. This may include diversifying investments, setting risk tolerance parameters, and regularly reviewing the trust's asset allocation strategy. Consider working with investment professionals who specialize in managing trust assets and have a thorough understanding of your business's financial objectives and risk profile.

Succession Planning for Trustee Roles:

Include succession planning provisions for trustee roles within the trust. Identify potential successor trustees and ensure that there is a smooth transition of responsibilities in the event of a trustee's incapacity, resignation, or death. Regularly review and update the succession plan to reflect changes in the trustee team or the availability of qualified individuals to fulfill the trustee's role.

Monitor Changes in Business and Legal

Landscape:

Stay informed about changes in the business and legal landscape that may impact the trust. This includes changes in business regulations, tax laws, and fiduciary responsibilities.

Regularly consult with your legal and financial advisors to ensure that the trust remains compliant with current laws and that its structure and provisions continue to align with your business goals.

Regular Trust Audits:

Consider conducting periodic audits of the trust's operations and financial activities. An independent review of the trust's performance and compliance can provide valuable insights and help identify any areas that require improvement or adjustment.

Educate Successors and Stakeholders:

Educate potential successors, beneficiaries, and

other stakeholders about the trust's purpose, provisions, and objectives. Provide them with the necessary information and resources to understand their roles and responsibilities within the trust structure.

Review Trustee Fees and Compensation:

Regularly review and assess the trustee fees and compensation structure to ensure that it remains fair and reasonable. Consider benchmarking against industry standards and engaging in discussions with the trustee team to maintain transparency and alignment.

Evaluate the Need for Professional Trust Administration:

As the trust grows in complexity or if your business requires specialized expertise, consider engaging professional trust administrators or corporate trustees to manage the trust's day-to-day operations. Professional administrators bring specialized knowledge, experience, and dedicated resources to ensure the effective administration and management of the trust. By following these additional steps in creating and managing a trust, you can enhance its effectiveness, protect the trust assets, and ensure that it continues to serve as a valuable tool for your business financing needs. Regular review and collaboration with professional advisors, and proactive management are key to maximizing the benefits and achieving your long-term financial objectives through the trust structure.

Review and Adjust Distribution Policies:

Regularly review and adjust the distribution policies of the trust to ensure they align with the changing needs and circumstances of the beneficiaries and the overall goals of the trust. Consider factors such as the financial needs of the beneficiaries, changes in their life situations, and any unexpected events that may require adjustments to the distribution strategy.

Monitor and Address Legal and Compliance Issues:

Stay vigilant in monitoring legal and compliance issues that may affect the trust. This includes changes in trust laws, fiduciary responsibilities, reporting requirements, and regulatory developments. Work closely with your legal and financial advisors to ensure that the trust remains in compliance with all applicable laws and regulations.

Maintain Proper Documentation and Recordkeeping:

Maintain accurate and up-to-date documentation and recordkeeping for the trust. This includes keeping track of all trust-related transactions, correspondence, financial statements, and legal documents. Proper documentation is crucial for transparency, compliance, and ensuring that the trust's activities can be readily reviewed and audited when necessary.

Review and Update Estate Planning:

Coordinate the trust with your overall estate planning strategy. Regularly review and update your estate planning documents to ensure that the trust provisions align with your broader estate planning goals. Consider any changes in your personal circumstances, family dynamics, or estate tax laws that may impact the effectiveness of the trust in achieving your estate planning objectives.

Evaluate Investment Performance:

Regularly evaluate the investment performance of the trust assets. Monitor the performance of the trust's investments, assess the risk-adjusted returns, and consider any necessary adjustments to the investment strategy.

Work closely with your investment advisors to ensure that the trust's assets are effectively allocated and managed to meet the long-term financial goals of the trust.

Plan for Contingencies:

Plan for contingencies that may arise during the life of the trust. Consider potential scenarios such as changes in the business landscape, economic downturns, or unforeseen events that may impact the trust's operations.

Develop contingency plans to address these scenarios, including alternative investment strategies, risk management measures, and succession plans for key roles within the trust.

Communicate and Engage with Beneficiaries:

Foster open communication and engagement with the beneficiaries of the trust. Keep them informed about the trust's activities, financial performance, and any changes or decisions that may affect them. Provide regular updates, hold beneficiary meetings, and address any questions or concerns they may have. Building a strong relationship with the beneficiaries helps ensure their understanding and support of the trust's objectives.

Maintain Confidentiality and Privacy:

Safeguard the confidentiality and privacy of the trust and its beneficiaries. Avoid disclosing sensitive information about the trust's operations or beneficiaries unless required by law or with the explicit consent of the parties involved. Maintain proper data security measures to protect the trust's information from unauthorized access or breaches.

Review and Update Trustee and Beneficiary Succession Plans:

Regularly review and update the trustee and beneficiary succession plans within the trust. Identify potential successor trustees and beneficiaries and ensure a smooth transition of responsibilities and rights when necessary.

Update the trust provisions to reflect any changes in the trustee or beneficiary structure, considering the best interests of the trust and the intentions of the settler.

Regularly Review Trust Performance Against Goals:

Regularly assess the trust's performance against its intended goals and objectives. Evaluate whether the trust is effectively meeting its intended purpose and supporting your business financing needs. Consider the trust's financial performance, tax efficiency, asset growth, and other relevant metrics to determine if any adjustments or improvements are necessary.

Monitor Changes in Tax Laws and Regulations:

Stay up to date with changes in tax laws and regulations that may impact the taxation of the trust and its beneficiaries. Work closely with your tax advisor to ensure that the trust's tax strategies remain compliant with the latest regulations and to identify any potential tax-saving opportunities. Regularly review the trust's tax filings and documentation to ensure accuracy and compliance with tax requirements.

Seek Professional Guidance for Complex Trust Matters:

For trusts with complex structures or significant assets, consider engaging specialized professionals who have expertise in trust administration, taxation, and legal matters. Seek the guidance of professionals such as trust officers, estate planning attorneys, and tax specialists who can provide expert advice and ensure the proper management of the trust.

Stay Informed About Changes in Trust Law:

Stay informed about changes in trust law that may impact the administration, management, or taxation of the trust.

Attend relevant seminars, conferences, or workshops to keep up with the latest developments in trust law and to gain insights from experts in the field. Consult with your legal advisor to ensure that the trust remains compliant with evolving trust laws and to explore any opportunities to optimize the trust's structure and benefits.

Conduct Periodic Trust Reviews:

Conduct periodic reviews of the trust's structure, provisions, and performance. Assess the trust's ongoing relevance and effectiveness in achieving your business financing objectives. Review the trust's investment strategy, asset allocation, and distribution policies to ensure they align with your business goals and the needs of the beneficiaries.

Adapt and Adjust Trust Strategies as Needed:

Be flexible and willing to adapt the trust's strategies as your business and financial circumstances change. Regularly reassess the trust's goals, objectives, and strategies to ensure they align with your evolving business financing needs. Seek advice from your professional advisors to identify opportunities for improvement and adjust the trust's strategies accordingly. In summary, creating and managing a trust for business financing requires ongoing diligence, proactive management, and collaboration with professional advisors. By following these steps, regularly reviewing the trust's performance, staying informed about legal and tax changes, and adapting strategies as needed, you can ensure that the trust remains a valuable tool for your business's financial stability and growth.

Chapter 5:

THE BENEFITS OF OFFSHORE BANKING

Offshore banking refers to the practice of keeping funds in a bank located outside one's home country. It has gained popularity among individuals and businesses seeking to diversify their financial holdings and enjoy various benefits that offshore banking can offer. In this chapter, we will explore the advantages of offshore banking and how it can contribute to your business financing strategies.

Financial Privacy and Confidentiality:

Offshore banking jurisdictions often provide a higher level of financial privacy and confidentiality compared to domestic banks. They have strict regulations and laws in place to protect the privacy of their clients' financial information. By banking offshore, you can enjoy an added layer of confidentiality, shielding your financial affairs from unnecessary scrutiny or unauthorized access.

Asset Protection:

Offshore banking can offer enhanced asset protection by keeping your funds in a jurisdiction with robust legal frameworks and favorable creditor protection laws.

In the event of a legal dispute or financial challenge, having assets held offshore can make it more difficult for creditors or litigants to seize or access those funds.

Diversification of Risk:

Offshore banking allows you to diversify your financial risk by holding assets in different jurisdictions and currencies. This diversification can help protect your business from potential economic or political instability in your home country. By spreading your financial assets across multiple jurisdictions, you reduce the risk of having all your eggs in one basket and increase the resilience of your business finances.

Tax Optimization:

Many offshore jurisdictions offer favorable tax regimes, including lower or zero tax rates on specific types of income or assets. By banking offshore, you can take advantage of these tax benefits to optimize your business's tax position. However, it is essential to ensure that you comply with the tax laws and regulations of both your home country and the offshore jurisdiction to maintain legal and ethical tax practices.

Foreign Currency Accounts:

Offshore banking enables you to hold accounts denominated in different currencies. This flexibility allows you to transact and hold funds in various currencies, mitigating the risk of currency fluctuations and facilitating international business operations. Foreign currency accounts can provide a convenient tool for managing foreign exchange risks and conducting cross-border transactions more efficiently.

Access to International Markets:

Offshore banking can provide access to international markets, investment opportunities, and financial services that may not be readily available in your home country. Offshore banks often have a global network of branches, facilitating cross-border transactions and investments. This access to international markets can broaden your investment options, diversify your portfolio, and open doors to new business ventures and partnerships.

Wealth Preservation and Estate Planning:

Offshore banking can be instrumental in wealth preservation and estate planning strategies. By holding assets offshore, you can protect and preserve your wealth for future generations.

Offshore jurisdictions often offer more flexible and favorable estate planning laws, enabling you to structure your assets in a way that minimizes inheritance taxes, facilitates smooth wealth transfer, and ensures the long-term financial security of your beneficiaries.

International Trade and Business Expansion:

For businesses engaged in international trade or considering expanding their operations globally, offshore banking can provide significant advantages.

Offshore banks can offer specialized trade finance solutions, such as letters of credit, documentary collections, and currency hedging, to facilitate international transactions and mitigate risks associated with cross-border trade. Offshore banking can also support business expansion by providing access to foreign capital markets, facilitating international payments, and offering tailored financial solutions for businesses operating in multiple jurisdictions.

Higher Interest Rates and Investment Opportunities:

Offshore banks may offer higher interest rates on deposits compared to domestic banks. This can potentially enhance the return on your business surplus funds and increase your overall investment yield. Additionally, offshore banking can provide access to a wider range of investment opportunities, including offshore mutual funds, hedge funds, and private equity funds, which may offer attractive returns and diversification benefits.

Flexible Banking Services:

Offshore banks often provide more personalized and flexible banking services, tailored to the needs of international clients and businesses. These services can include multi-currency accounts, international wire transfers, online banking platforms, wealth management services, and dedicated relationship managers who understand the unique requirements of offshore clients.

It is important to note that while offshore banking can offer various benefits, it is crucial to engage in responsible and legal practices. Ensure that you comply with all applicable tax laws and regulations, report your offshore holdings as required, and work with reputable financial institutions and advisors to navigate the complexities of offshore banking. In conclusion, offshore banking can be a valuable component of your business financing strategy, offering financial privacy, asset protection, tax optimization, diversification, and access to international markets. By exploring the benefits of offshore banking and understanding how it aligns with your business objectives, you can make informed decisions to optimize your financial position and drive business growth.

Chapter 6

BUILDING A STRONG FINANCIAL FOUNDATION

Building a strong financial foundation is essential for the success and sustainability of any business. It involves establishing sound financial practices, managing cash flow effectively, and making strategic decisions to ensure long-term financial stability. In this chapter, we will delve into key strategies for building a strong financial foundation for your business.

Develop a Comprehensive Financial Plan:

Start by creating a comprehensive financial plan that outlines your business's financial goals, objectives, and strategies. Identify key financial metrics, such as revenue targets, profit margins, and cash flow projections, and establish a timeline for achieving them. Consider factors such as market conditions, industry trends, and competitive dynamics when formulating your financial plan.

Implement Effective Budgeting and Expense Management:

Develop a budget that aligns with your financial plan and sets realistic targets for revenue generation and expense management. Monitor and control expenses carefully, identifying areas where costs can be reduced or optimized without compromising the quality of products or services. Regularly review your budget and adjust it as needed to reflect changes in market conditions or business priorities.

Establish Robust Cash Flow Management:

Cash flow management is crucial for maintaining a healthy financial foundation. Ensure that your business has sufficient cash flow to cover operational expenses, debt obligations, and future investments. Monitor cash flow regularly, forecasting inflows and outflows to identify potential shortfalls or surpluses. Implement strategies to improve cash flow, such as offering incentives for early customer payments, negotiating favorable payment terms with suppliers, and managing inventory levels efficiently.

Maintain Adequate Working Capital:

Adequate working capital is essential for day-to-day operations and business growth. Strive to maintain a healthy balance between current assets and liabilities to meet short-term financial obligations.

Consider financing options, such as lines of credit or business loans, to bridge any temporary gaps in working capital requirements. Regularly assess and optimize your working capital cycle by minimizing inventory holding periods, negotiating favorable payment terms with suppliers, and accelerating the collection of accounts receivable.

Manage Debt Responsibly:

Debt can be a useful tool for financing business operations and growth. However, it should be managed responsibly to avoid excessive debt burdens and financial strain. Evaluate the cost and terms of borrowing carefully, considering factors such as interest rates, repayment schedules, and collateral requirements.

Develop a debt repayment plan and make consistent and timely payments to maintain a good credit rating and financial credibility.

Implement Strong Internal Controls:

Establish strong internal controls to safeguard your business's financial assets and minimize the risk of fraud or mismanagement. Implement segregation of duties, ensuring that different individuals are responsible for key financial functions, such as handling cash, recording transactions, and reconciling accounts. Conduct regular internal audits and reviews to identify any weaknesses or vulnerabilities in your financial processes and make necessary improvements.

Invest in Financial Management Systems:

Implement robust financial management systems and software to streamline financial processes, track financial performance, and generate accurate and timely reports.

Choose systems that integrate key functions such as accounting, invoicing, budgeting, and financial analysis to improve efficiency and decision-making.

Train employees on how to use the financial management systems effectively and encourage regular utilization of the tools and reports provided.

Build Strong Relationships with Financial Partners:

Cultivate strong relationships with financial

partners, such as banks, lenders, and investors.

Regularly communicate with your financial partners, providing them with accurate and up-to-date financial information and discussing your business's financial performance and future. Building trust and transparency with financial partners can lead to improved access to financing, favorable terms, and valuable advice and support.

Continuously Monitor and Evaluate Financial Performance:

Monitor your business's financial performance regularly, comparing actual results against your financial plan and key performance indicators. Identify areas of improvement and take corrective actions promptly to address any financial challenges or deviations from your plan.

Conduct periodic financial reviews and evaluations to assess the effectiveness of your financial strategies and adjust as needed.

Seek Professional Financial Advice:

Consider engaging the services of professional financial advisors, such as accountants, financial planners, or business consultants. Seek their expertise and guidance in areas such as tax planning, investment strategies, risk management, and financial decision-making.

Professional advice can provide valuable insights and help you make informed financial decisions that align with your business goals. By implementing these strategies, you can establish a strong financial foundation for your business. Building a solid financial framework will not only ensure stability but also position your business for growth, profitability, and long-term success.

Chapter 7

Managing Financial Risks

In business, managing financial risks is crucial for protecting your assets, ensuring stability, and mitigating potential financial setbacks. By identifying, assessing, and implementing strategies to manage financial risks, you can safeguard your business's financial well-being and enhance your chances of success. In this chapter, we will explore key strategies for effectively managing financial risks.

Identify Financial Risks:

Start by identifying the potential financial risks your business may face. These risks can vary depending on factors such as industry, market conditions, and the nature of your business operations. Common financial risks include market volatility, credit risk, liquidity risk, operational risk, foreign exchange risk, interest rate risk, and regulatory compliance risk.

Assess and Prioritize Risks:

Once you have identified potential risks, assess their likelihood of occurrence and potential impact on your business. Prioritize risks based on their significance and the level of potential damage they can cause to your business's financial health.

Develop Risk Management Strategies:

Develop risk management strategies to mitigate or minimize the impact of identified risks. These strategies may include:

Risk Avoidance:

If a risk poses a significant threat and is avoidable, consider avoiding or eliminating it altogether. For example, if a particular market segment is highly volatile and poses a significant financial risk, you may choose to avoid or minimize your exposure to that segment.

Risk Transfer:

Transfer the financial risk to another party through mechanisms such as insurance policies, hedging instruments, or outsourcing certain functions to external service providers.

Risk Reduction:

Implement measures to reduce the likelihood or impact of identified risks. For example, if liquidity risk is a concern, you can implement cash flow management strategies, maintain adequate working capital, or establish lines of credit for emergency funding.

Risk Diversification:

Diversify your business's financial resources, investments, and customer base to reduce dependence on any single factor or entity. This can help mitigate the impact of specific risks and enhance overall resilience. Risk Monitoring and Contingency Planning: Continuously monitor and assess the effectiveness of risk management strategies. Develop contingency plans to respond swiftly and effectively if identified risks materialize.

Implement Internal Controls:

Implement robust internal controls to mitigate the risk of fraud, financial mismanagement, or unauthorized activities. Establish clear policies and procedures for financial transactions, segregation of duties, and regular financial reporting and monitoring. Regularly review and assess the effectiveness of internal controls and make necessary improvements.

Maintain Adequate Insurance Coverage:

Assess your business's insurance needs and ensure that you have appropriate coverage to protect against potential financial risks. Common types of insurance coverage include general liability insurance, property insurance, professional liability insurance, and business interruption insurance. Regularly review your insurance policies to ensure they are up to date and provide adequate protection based on the evolving needs of your business.

Stay Informed and Engage Professional Advice:

Stay informed about market trends, regulatory changes, and emerging financial risks relevant to your business.

Engage the services of financial advisors, risk management professionals, or industry experts who can provide guidance and advice on managing specific financial risks.

Regularly Review and Update Risk Management Strategies:

Financial risks can evolve over time, so it is crucial to regularly review and update your risk management strategies. Assess the effectiveness of your existing strategies, identify new risks that may have emerged, and adjust your risk management approach accordingly.

By implementing these strategies, you can effectively manage financial risks and protect your business's financial stability. Remember that risk management is an ongoing process that requires vigilance, adaptability, and a proactive approach. Regularly review and update your risk management strategies to align with changing business dynamics and ensure the continued success and resilience of your business.

Chapter 8

FINANCING ALTERNATIVES FOR BUSINESS GROWTH

Business growth often requires additional financing to support expansion, new initiatives, or investment in resources. While traditional financing options, such as bank loans, are commonly used, there are alternative sources of funding available that can provide unique advantages for businesses. In this chapter, we will explore various financing alternatives to fuel your business growth.

Venture Capital:

Venture capital involves obtaining funding from investors in exchange for equity or a share in the business. Venture capitalists typically invest in early-stage or high-growth companies with substantial growth potential. Beyond financial support, venture capitalists often provide valuable expertise, industry connections, and guidance to help businesses succeed.

Angel Investors:

Angel investors are individuals who invest their own capital in businesses in exchange for equity. They are typically high-net-worth individuals who offer financial support and mentorship to startups or small businesses.

Angel investors can provide valuable funding, industry knowledge, and networks to help accelerate business growth.

Crowdfunding:

Crowdfunding involves raising funds from many individuals, typically through an online platform.

There are different types of crowdfunding, including donation-based, reward-based, equity-based, and debt-based crowdfunding. Crowdfunding allows businesses to tap into a wide network of potential investors and supporters while raising capital for specific projects or business expansion.

Peer to peer Lending:

Peer to peer lending platforms connect borrowers directly with individual lenders. This alternative financing option bypasses traditional financial institutions, allowing businesses to access funding from individual investors. Peer to peer lending can provide faster approval times, flexible terms, and competitive interest rates compared to traditional loans.

Invoice Financing:

Invoice financing, also known as accounts receivable financing, allows businesses to obtain funds by using their outstanding customer invoices as collateral.

This financing option provides businesses with immediate cash flow by leveraging their unpaid invoices. Invoice financing can help address cash flow gaps and provide working capital to support business growth.

Asset-Based Lending:

Asset-based lending involves using a company's assets, such as inventory, equipment, or accounts receivable, as collateral for obtaining financing. This type of financing can be particularly beneficial for businesses with valuable assets but limited access to traditional financing options.

Asset-based lending provides businesses with a flexible and scalable source of capital to support expansion or operational needs.

Grants and Subsidies:

Government grants and subsidies are financial assistance programs offered by governmental bodies to support specific industries, projects, or initiatives. These programs can provide non-repayable funds or low-interest loans to eligible businesses. Research and identify relevant grants and subsidies that align with your business's goals and initiatives.

Strategic Partnerships and Joint Ventures:

Forming strategic partnerships or joint ventures with other businesses can provide access to funding, resources, expertise, and market opportunities. By leveraging the strengths and synergies of multiple entities, businesses can accelerate growth and achieve shared objectives.

Business Incubators and Accelerators:

Business incubators and accelerators are programs that provide support, mentorship, and often financial assistance to early-stage startups. These programs offer access to networks, resources, and funding opportunities to help businesses grow rapidly. Participating in an incubator or accelerator can provide valuable guidance and exposure to investors.

Government and Nonprofit Organizations:

Explore financing options provided by government agencies, economic development organizations, and nonprofit entities. These organizations may offer loans, grants, or subsidized financing programs designed to promote business growth and economic development.

It is important to thoroughly evaluate each financing alternative based on your business's specific needs and goals. Consider factors such as the terms and conditions, interest rates or equity requirements, repayment terms, and the potential impact on your business's ownership and control when pursuing alternative financing options, keep the following tips in mind:

Research and Due Diligence:

Conduct thorough research on potential investors, crowdfunding platforms, or financing programs.

Evaluate their track record, reputation, and

compatibility with your business's industry and growth objectives.

Review the terms and conditions, fees, and any legal or contractual obligations associated with the financing option.

Prepare a Strong Business Case:

Clearly articulate your business's growth plans, market potential, and competitive advantage to potential investors or lenders. Develop a compelling business plan and financial projections that demonstrate the viability and profitability of your business. Highlight the unique value proposition and growth prospects that make your business an attractive investment opportunity.

Seek Professional Advice:

Engage with financial advisors, attorneys, or consultants who specialize in alternative financing options. They can provide guidance on the legal and regulatory aspects, help negotiate favorable terms, and ensure you make informed decisions.

Maintain Transparency and Communication:

Be transparent and provide accurate and up to date information to potential investors or lenders. Communicate openly about your business's progress, challenges, and plans for growth. Establish a strong relationship based on trust and regular communication to build confidence and support from financing partners.

Understand the Implications:

Consider the long-term implications of the financing option for your business. Assess the impact on ownership, control, and decision-making. Evaluate the potential benefits and risks associated with the financing alternative and how it aligns with your overall business strategy.

Evaluate Cost vs. Benefit:

Compare the costs associated with the alternative financing option to the potential benefits it offers. Assess the return on investment, the value of additional resources or expertise gained, and the impact on your business's growth trajectory. Remember that alternative financing options may have different requirements, timelines, and levels of complexity compared to traditional financing methods. It is essential to carefully assess each option, consider the specific needs of your business and align them with your growth objectives. By exploring and utilizing alternative financing options, you can access additional capital, expertise, and resources to fuel your business's growth and maximize its potential for success. However, always approach alternative financing with a well-informed and cautious mindset, ensuring that the terms and conditions align with your long-term vision and financial objectives.

Chapter 9

TRADITIONAL FINANCING OPTIONS FOR BUSINESS

Traditional financing options, such as bank loans, remain a popular choice for businesses seeking funding. These options offer stability, established structures, and competitive interest rates. In this chapter, we will delve into various traditional financing options available to businesses.

Bank Loans:

Bank loans are one of the most common forms of financing for businesses. They involve borrowing a specific amount of money from a bank, which is then repaid with interest over an agreed-upon term. Bank loans can be used for various purposes, including working capital, equipment purchase, or expansion projects.

They typically require collateral and may involve strict lending criteria and documentation.

Business Lines of Credit:

A business line of credit provides a flexible and revolving source of funds that businesses can access as needed. Like a credit card, businesses can draw from the line of credit up to a predetermined limit and repay the borrowed amount with interest. Lines of credit are useful for managing short-term cash flow gaps, seasonal fluctuations, or unexpected expenses.

Trade Credit:

Trade credit is a financing arrangement with suppliers or vendors that allows businesses to purchase goods or services on credit terms. It offers a temporary extension of payment terms, typically ranging from 30 to 90 days, giving businesses time to generate revenue from the goods or services before payment is due. Trade credit can help improve cash flow and provide working capital for day-to-day operations.

Equipment Financing:

Equipment financing enables businesses to acquire necessary equipment without making a large upfront payment. Lenders provide funds to purchase the equipment, and the equipment itself serves as collateral. The loan is repaid over a specified period, usually matching the expected useful life of the equipment.

Commercial Mortgages:

Commercial mortgages are loans used to finance the purchase or renovation of commercial properties, such as office buildings, retail spaces, or warehouses. These loans are secured by the property itself, and repayment terms can extend over a long period, typically 10 to 30 years. Commercial mortgages offer lower interest rates compared to other forms of financing and can provide stability and long-term financing for real estate investments.

Small Business Administration (SBA) Loans:

The U.S. Small Business Administration (SBA) offers various loan programs designed to support small businesses. SBA loans are partially guaranteed by the SBA, reducing the risk for lenders, and making them more accessible to businesses that may not qualify for conventional loans. These loans can be used for a range of purposes, including working capital, equipment purchases, or business acquisition.

Factoring:

Factoring is a financing option where businesses sell their accounts receivable to a third-party (a factor) at a discount. The factor advances a portion of the invoice value to the business, providing immediate cash flow.

The factor assumes responsibility for collecting payment from customers and deducts a fee for the service.

Grants and Government Programs:

Government agencies and nonprofit organizations offer grants and financing programs to support specific industries, research and development, or community initiatives. These programs provide non-repayable funds or low-interest loans to eligible businesses. Research available grants and government programs that align with your business's objectives and criteria.

When considering traditional financing options, it's important to assess the terms, interest rates, repayment periods, and eligibility criteria. Prepare a strong business plan, financial statements, and supporting documentation to demonstrate your business's creditworthiness and ability to repay the loan. Consult with your financial advisor or banker to understand the options available and select the most suitable financing option for your business's needs.

Remember, traditional financing options may involve more stringent requirements and longer processing times compared to alternative financing options. However, they offer stability, established relationships with financial institutions, and access to competitive interest rates. Assess

your business's financial situation, cash flow projections, and long-term goals to determine the best traditional financing option for your business's growth and success.

Chapter 10
Navigating the Financing Process

Obtaining financing for your business can be a complex and challenging process. It requires careful planning, thorough preparation, and effective communication with potential lenders or investors. In this chapter, we will guide you through the steps of navigating the financing process.

Assess Your Financing Needs:

Start by evaluating your business's financial requirements. Determine the purpose of the financing, whether it's for working capital, expansion, equipment purchase, or other specific needs. Conduct a detailed analysis of the amount of funding required and the timeframe within which you need the funds.

Develop a Comprehensive Business Plan:

A well-crafted business plan is crucial when seeking financing. Your business plan should include a detailed description of your business, market analysis, competition, marketing strategy, financial projections, and an explanation of how the funding will be used.

Be sure to highlight the unique value proposition of your business and the potential for growth and profitability.

Organize Your Financial Documents:

Lenders and investors will require detailed financial information to assess your business's creditworthiness and repayment capacity. Prepare financial statements, including balance sheets, income statements, and cash flow statements. Gather tax returns, bank statements, and any other relevant financial documents.

Ensure that your financial records are accurate, up-to-date, and well organized.

Research Potential Financing Sources:

Identify potential lenders or investors that align with your business's financing needs and objectives. Research their lending criteria, interest rates, terms, and industry focus.

Consider reaching out to your existing banking relationships or exploring alternative funding sources, such as angel investors or venture capital firms.

Prepare a Loan Proposal or Investment Pitch:

Craft a compelling loan proposal or investment pitch to present to potential lenders or investors. Clearly articulate your business's unique selling points, growth potential, and the benefits of financing your business.

Present a solid repayment plan or exit strategy to demonstrate how the lender or investor will recoup their investment.

Build Relationships:

Establish relationships with potential lenders or

investors before seeking financing by attending industry events, networking functions, or investor pitch competitions to connect with relevant stakeholders. Cultivate relationships based on trust, credibility, and mutual understanding.

Submit Applications and Documentation:

Complete the necessary loan applications or investment documentation. Ensure that all required forms, supporting documents, and financial statements are included. Pay attention to the details and follow the instructions provided by the lender or investor.

Be Prepared for Due Diligence:

Lenders and investors will conduct due diligence to evaluate the risks and potential returns of financing your business. Be prepared to provide additional information, answer questions, and provide access to your business's financial and operational data.

Negotiate Terms and Conditions:

If you receive financing offers, carefully review the terms and conditions. Negotiate when appropriate, seeking terms that are favorable and align with your business's needs and goals. Consult with your legal and financial advisors to ensure you understand the implications of the financing agreement.

Close the Financing Deal:

Once you have selected a financing option and negotiated the terms, it's time to close the deal. Review all final documents, seek legal counsel if necessary, and sign the agreement. Be sure to comply with any post-funding requirements, such as reporting or monitoring obligations.

Maintain Open Communication:

Keep the lines of communication open with your lender or investors. Provide regular updates on your business's progress, financial performance, and any significant developments.

Timely and transparent communication can help foster a positive relationship and address any concerns or issues that may arise. Remember, navigating the financing process requires persistence, patience, and preparation. Be proactive in seeking financing opportunities, maintain accurate financial records, and continuously refine your business plan. By demonstrating your business's potential and aligning it with the right financing sources, you can secure the funding needed to fuel growth and achieve your business goals.

Chapter 11
Managing Business Finances

Once you have secured financing for your business, it is essential to effectively manage your finances to ensure long-term success. Proper financial management allows you to make informed decisions, track performance, and maintain a healthy cash flow. In this chapter, we will explore key strategies for managing your business finances.

Create a Financial Plan:

Develop a comprehensive financial plan that outlines your short-term and long-term financial goals. Identify key performance indicators (KPIs) that align with your business objectives and track them regularly. Set realistic revenue and expense targets and regularly review and adjust your plan as needed.

Maintain Accurate Financial Records:

Establish a system for maintaining accurate financial records, including bookkeeping, accounting software, or professional assistance.

Track income, expenses, and cash flow on a regular basis to gain insights into your business's financial health. Ensure that all financial transactions are properly recorded and reconciled.

Monitor Cash Flow:

Cash flow management is crucial for the sustainability of your business. Develop cash flow projections to anticipate inflows and outflows of cash. Regularly review your cash flow statement to identify potential gaps or surpluses.

Implement strategies to improve cash flow, such as optimizing payment terms with suppliers, managing inventory levels, or offering incentives for early customer payments.

Control Costs:

Keep a close eye on your expenses and implement cost-control measures. Regularly review your budget and identify areas where costs can be reduced or optimized. Negotiate favorable terms with vendors and suppliers and explore bulk purchasing or cost-saving alternatives.

Monitor and Manage Debt:

If your business has taken on debt, monitor and manage it effectively. Make timely loan or credit card payments to maintain a good credit history. Consider refinancing options if it can help lower interest rates or improve cash flow. Avoid excessive debt that may strain your business's financial position.

Implement Effective Financial Controls:

Establish internal controls to protect your business from fraud, errors, or misuse of funds. Implement segregation of duties, review financial reports regularly, and perform periodic audits. Use financial management tools and software to automate processes and ensure accuracy.

Regularly Review and Analyze Financial Reports:

Regularly review financial reports such as income statements, balance sheets, and cash flow statements. Analyze financial ratios and trends to gain insights into your business's financial performance. Compare your actual results to your financial plan and adjust your strategies accordingly.

Seek Professional Financial Advice:

Engage with a financial advisor or accountant to gain expert insights into managing your business finances. They can provide guidance on financial planning, tax strategies, and compliance with regulatory requirements. Regularly consult with your financial advisor to stay updated on industry trends and changes that may impact your business.

Plan for Contingencies:

Anticipate and plan for unexpected events or emergencies that may impact your business finances. Maintain an emergency fund to cover unforeseen expenses or economic downturns. Explore insurance options to protect your business from potential risks.

Continuously Educate Yourself:

Stay informed about financial management best practices, industry trends, and regulatory changes. Attend workshops, seminars, or webinars related to financial management and business finance.

Continuously improve your financial literacy to make informed decisions and adapt to changing circumstances. Effective financial management is vital for the long-term success of your business. By implementing these strategies and regularly monitoring your financial performance, you can maintain a healthy financial position, make informed decisions, and navigate potential challenges. Remember, financial management is an ongoing process that requires dedication and adaptability to ensure the financial stability and growth of your business.

Chapter 12

Evaluating and Adjusting Your Financing Strategy

As your business evolves, it's crucial to periodically evaluate and adjust your financing strategy. The financing needs of your business may change over time, and staying proactive in assessing and optimizing your financing options can help you maintain a competitive edge. In this chapter, we will explore the key considerations for evaluating and adjusting your financing strategy.

Assess Your Current Financing:

Start by evaluating your existing financing arrangements, including loans, lines of credit, or other forms of funding. Review the terms, interest rates, repayment schedules, and any associated fees. Determine whether your current financing aligns with your business goals and financial needs. Identify Financing Gaps or Opportunities: Conduct a thorough analysis of your business's financial position and future funding requirements. Identify any financing gaps or areas where additional funding may be beneficial. Consider factors such as working capital needs, expansion plans, equipment upgrades, or market opportunities.

Explore Alternative Financing Options:

Research and explore alternative financing options beyond traditional bank loans. Investigate options such as crowdfunding, peer to peer lending, invoice financing, or merchant cash advances. Each financing option has its own advantages and considerations, so evaluate them based on your specific needs and risk tolerance.

Review Tax Incentives and Grants:

Stay updated on tax incentives, grants, or

government programs that may be applicable to your business. Research and assess eligibility criteria, application processes, and potential benefits. These incentives can help offset costs and provide additional funding for specific initiatives or investments.

Consult with Financial Professionals:

Seek guidance from financial advisors, accountants, or consultants who specialize in business financing.

They can provide valuable insights and help you evaluate the feasibility and implications of different financing options. Work collaboratively with them to develop a financing strategy that aligns with your business objectives.

Consider the Cost of Financing:

Evaluate the cost of financing, including interest rates, fees, and other charges. Compare different financing options to determine the most cost-effective solution for your business. Consider the impact of financing costs on your overall profitability and cash flow.

Revisit Your Business Plan and Financial Projections:

Regularly review and update your business plan and financial projections to reflect any changes in your financing strategy. Ensure that your financing aligns with your long-term goals and growth plans. Adjust your financial projections accordingly to reflect the anticipated impact of new financing arrangements.

Mitigate Risks:

Evaluate the risks associated with different financing options. Consider factors such as interest rate fluctuations, collateral requirements, or potential changes in repayment terms. Develop risk mitigation strategies to safeguard your business's financial stability.

Maintain Strong Relationships with Lenders and

Investors:

Nurture relationships with your existing lenders or investors. Regularly communicate with them, provide updates on your business's performance, and address any concerns. Strong relationships can help you negotiate better terms, access additional funding when needed, or explore new financing opportunities.

Stay Informed about Financing Trends:

Keep abreast of the latest financing trends, industry developments, and market conditions. Attend industry conferences, workshops, or webinars to stay informed about emerging financing options or innovative approaches. Networking with peers and industry experts can provide valuable insights into financing strategies. Evaluating and adjusting your financing strategy is an ongoing process that should be conducted at regular intervals. By regularly assessing your financing needs, exploring alternative options, and staying proactive in adapting your strategy, you can optimize your business's financing to support growth, innovation, and long-term success.

Chapter 13
MAINTAINING FINANCIAL DISCIPLINE AND SUSTAINABILITY

Building and maintaining financial discipline is crucial for the long-term sustainability and success of your business. It involves adopting sound financial practices, managing risks, and making informed decisions to ensure the financial health and stability of your company. In this chapter, we will explore key strategies for maintaining financial discipline and sustainability.

Implement Effective Budgeting:

Develop a comprehensive budget that aligns with your business goals and objectives. Track and control expenses, ensuring they are in line with your budgetary allocations. Regularly review your budget and adjust as necessary to optimize resource allocation.

Monitor Key Financial Metrics:

Identify and monitor key financial metrics that provide insights into your business's performance. Examples include revenue growth, gross margin, net profit margin, return on investment (ROI), and working capital ratio.

Set targets for these metrics and regularly review and analyze them to gauge your business's financial health.

Maintain Healthy Cash Flow:

Cash flow management is crucial for day-to-day operations and financial stability. Monitor and forecast cash flow regularly to ensure sufficient liquidity to meet obligations. Implement strategies to improve cash flow, such as optimizing inventory management, negotiating

favorable payment terms and incentivizing timely customer payments.

Control and Minimize Debt:

Maintain a prudent approach to borrowing and manage debt effectively. Regularly review your debt structure and repayment obligations. Aim to minimize high-interest debt and explore opportunities to refinance or consolidate existing debt.

Build Reserves and Emergency Funds:

Set aside reserves and emergency funds to handle unexpected expenses or economic downturns.

Maintain a cash buffer to mitigate risks and maintain financial stability during challenging times.

Determine an appropriate amount based on your business's size, industry, and risk profile.

Continuously Monitor and Evaluate Costs:

Regularly review your cost structure to identify opportunities for cost optimization. Identify areas where expenses can be reduced without compromising the quality or efficiency of operations. Consider leveraging technology or outsourcing certain functions to lower costs.

Diversify Revenue Streams:

Relying heavily on a single revenue source can pose risks to your business's financial sustainability. Explore opportunities to diversify your revenue streams and reduce dependency on a single customer, product, or market.

Identify new markets, target different customer segments, or develop new products or services to expand your revenue base.

Conduct Scenario Planning and Risk Management:

Anticipate and plan for potential risks that could impact your business's financial sustainability. Conduct scenario planning exercises to assess the potential impact of external factors, such as economic changes or industry disruptions. Develop risk mitigation strategies and contingency plans to minimize the negative effects of unforeseen events. Invest in Financial Education and Expertise: Continuously invest in financial education to enhance your understanding of financial management principles and practices. Consider working with financial advisors, accountants, or consultants to gain expert insights and guidance. Regularly engage in professional development to stay updated on financial trends, regulations, and best practices.

Foster a Culture of Financial Discipline:

Promote a culture of financial discipline and responsibility throughout your organization. Ensure that all employees understand the importance of sound financial management practices. Provide training and resources to empower employees to make informed financial decisions in their respective roles. Maintaining financial discipline and sustainability requires a proactive and disciplined approach. By implementing these strategies, you can strengthen your business's financial position, mitigate risks, and position your company for long-term success. Remember, financial discipline is an ongoing commitment that requires consistent monitoring, evaluation, and adaptation to changing circumstances.

Chapter 14

ADAPTING TO CHANGING FINANCIAL LANDSCAPES

The financial landscape is constantly evolving, influenced by economic conditions, technological advancements, regulatory changes, and market trends. To navigate these changes successfully, businesses must be adaptable and responsive. In this chapter, we will explore strategies for adapting to changing financial landscapes and staying ahead of the curve.

Stay Abreast of Economic and Market Trends:

Regularly monitor economic indicators, market trends, and industry developments. Stay informed about changes that may impact on your business's financial landscape. Read industry publications, attend conferences, and engage in networking to gain insights and stay ahead of the curve.

Embrace Technological Advancements:

Leverage technology to streamline financial processes and improve efficiency. Adopt accounting software, financial management tools, and analytics platforms to automate tasks and gain real-time insights.

Explore emerging technologies such as blockchain, artificial intelligence, or robotic process automation to enhance financial operations.

Assess and Embrace Regulatory Changes:

Keep up to date with regulatory changes that impact on your business and the financial industry. Regularly review and assess how these changes affect your financial strategies, compliance requirements, and reporting obligations. Consult with legal and financial experts to ensure your business remains compliant with applicable regulations.

Continuously Review and Adapt Financing

Strategies:

Evaluate and adjust your financing strategies to align with changing financial landscapes. Explore new financing options, such as alternative lenders, crowdfunding, or venture capital, to capitalize on emerging trends.

Consider refinancing existing debt or renegotiating terms to take advantage of favorable market conditions.

Emphasize Financial Agility:

Foster a culture of financial agility within your organization. Encourage open communication, collaboration, and innovative thinking to respond quickly to changing financial landscapes. Establish processes for regular financial review and analysis to identify potential risks and opportunities.

Engage in Scenario Planning:

Develop scenario planning exercises to assess

the potential impact of different financial scenarios on your business. Consider best-case, worst-case, and moderate-case scenarios to evaluate the resilience of your financial strategies. Identify potential risks and develop contingency plans to mitigate their impact.

Foster Strategic Partnerships:

Cultivate relationships with strategic partners, including financial institutions, investors, and industry peers.

Collaborate with these partners to navigate changing financial landscapes, access new opportunities, and share best practices. Leverage their expertise and networks to gain insights into emerging trends and innovative financial solutions.

Encourage Continuous Learning and Development:

Promote a learning culture within your organization, encouraging employees to stay updated on financial trends and industry developments. Provide training and professional development opportunities to enhance financial literacy and expertise. Encourage employees to share knowledge and ideas that can help adapt to changing financial landscapes.

Monitor Competitive Landscape:

Keep a close eye on your competitors and their financial strategies. Analyze their financial performance, market positioning, and funding sources. Benchmark your business against industry peers to identify areas for improvement and innovation.

Be Open to Change and Innovation:

Embrace a mindset of continuous improvement and innovation. Be open to exploring new financial models, technologies, and approaches. Encourage experimentation and learn from failures to drive innovation and adaptability. Adapting to changing financial landscapes requires vigilance, agility, and a proactive mindset. By staying informed, embracing technology, adjusting financing strategies, and fostering a culture of innovation, your business can navigate and thrive in dynamic financial environments. Remember, adaptability is a key competitive advantage in today's rapidly changing business landscape.

Chapter 15

ALTERNATIVE FINANCING STRATEGIES

In addition to traditional financing options such as bank loans and lines of credit, businesses today have access to a wide range of alternative financing strategies. These strategies provide innovative ways to secure capital, diversify funding sources, and meet specific financial needs. In this chapter, we will explore some popular alternative financing strategies and their benefits.

Crowdfunding:

Crowdfunding involves raising funds from many individuals, typically through online platforms. There are different types of crowdfunding, including rewards-based crowdfunding, equity crowdfunding, and peer to peer lending.

Benefits:

Access to a larger pool of potential investors or supporters. Ability to validate product or business ideas through market demand. Opportunity to build a community of loyal customers or advocates.

Peer to peer (P2P) Lending:

P2P lending platforms connect borrowers directly with individual lenders. Borrowers create a profile and loan request, and lenders choose which loans to fund.

Benefits:

Simplified application process and faster funding compared to traditional lenders.

Potential for competitive interest rates based on creditworthiness. Flexibility in loan terms and repayment schedules.

Invoice Financing:

Invoice financing allows businesses to access

funds by selling their outstanding invoices to a third-party financing company. The financing company advances a percentage of the invoice value and collects the full payment from the customer.

Benefits:

Improved cash flow by converting accounts receivable into immediate working capital.

Reduced risk of lateness or non-payment from customers. Access to funds without taking on additional debt.

Merchant Cash Advances:

Merchant cash advances provide businesses with upfront funds in exchange for a percentage of future credit card or debit card sales. Repayment is made through a fixed percentage deducted from daily sales.

Benefits:

Quick access to funds with minimal

documentation and credit requirements. Repayment flexibility based on sales volume. Suitable for businesses with fluctuating sales volumes.

Revenue-Based Financing:

Revenue-based financing involves obtaining capital in exchange for a percentage of

future revenues. Payments are based on a fixed percentage of monthly revenues until a predetermined repayment cap is reached.

Benefits:

Repayment is tied to business performance, making it suitable for businesses with variable cash flows. No fixed repayment amounts, providing flexibility during slower periods. Potential for faster funding compared to traditional loan applications.

Asset-Based Lending:

Asset-based lending involves using company

assets, such as inventory, equipment, or accounts receivable, as collateral for a loan. The loan amount is determined based on the appraised value of the assets.

Benefits:

Access to funding based on the value of existing assets, even if the business has limited credit history. Flexibility in the use of funds, as asset-based loans can be used for various purposes. Potential for higher loan amounts compared to unsecured loans.

Venture Capital and Angel Investors:

Venture capital firms and angel investors provide equity financing to high-growth potential businesses in exchange for ownership stakes. They often provide expertise, mentorship, and industry connections in addition to capital.

Benefits:

Significant funding for businesses with high growth potential. Access to expertise, industry networks, and strategic guidance. Validation of business model and market potential.

Grants and Government Funding:

Grants and government funding programs provide non-repayable funds to businesses that meet specific eligibility criteria. These programs are often targeted towards specific industries, research and development, or social impact initiatives.

Benefits:

Access to capital without the need for repayment. Support for innovation, research, and development. Recognition and validation of projects with societal or environmental benefits.

Strategic Partnerships and Joint Ventures:

Strategic partnerships and joint ventures involve collaborating with other businesses to access funding, resources, and expertise. These partnerships can be structured in various ways, such as revenue-sharing agreements or shared investment opportunities.

Benefits:

Shared financial risks and responsibilities.

Access to additional capital, resources, and customer bases. Opportunities for knowledge exchange, innovation, and market expansion.

Family and Friends Financing:

Family and friends can provide informal financing by investing in or lending money to the business. This approach typically involves personal relationships and may have flexible terms and repayment arrangements.

Benefits:

Access to capital from individuals who believe in the business and its founders. Potential for more flexible terms and repayment schedules.

Opportunity to build stronger personal relationships while securing funding. When considering alternative financing strategies, it's essential to evaluate the specific needs and goals of your business. Each option comes with its own advantages, considerations, and risks. Carefully assess the terms, costs, and compatibility of each strategy with your business model before deciding. Additionally, consult with financial advisors or experts to ensure you make informed choices that align with your long-term financial objectives.

Chapter 16

ASSESSING THE RISKS OF ALTERNATIVE FINANCING

While alternative financing strategies offer various benefits and opportunities for businesses, it is important to assess and understand the associated risks. As with any financial decision, there are potential drawbacks and challenges that businesses must consider. In this chapter, we will explore the common risks of alternative financing and strategies for mitigating them.

Higher Costs:

Alternative financing options may come with higher interest rates, fees, or equity stakes compared to traditional financing.

Mitigation Strategies:

Carefully evaluate the overall cost of financing,

including interest rates, fees, and equity dilution, to ensure it aligns with the expected benefits. Compare different financing options to find the most cost-effective solution. Negotiate terms and conditions to secure more favorable rates or minimize equity dilution.

Limited Availability:

Some alternative financing options may have limited availability, especially for businesses with unique needs or in niche industries.

Mitigation Strategies:

Research and explore a wide range of alternative financing options to find the ones that best match your business needs. Build relationships with multiple financing providers to increase your chances of finding suitable options. Consider a combination of alternative financing strategies to diversify your funding sources.

Lack of Scalability:

Certain alternative financing methods, such as crowdfunding or grants, may have limitations on the amount of capital that can be raised.

Mitigation Strategies:

Assess your long-term funding needs and growth plans to determine if alternative financing options can meet your scalability requirements. Explore a combination of traditional and alternative financing to ensure access to sufficient capital as your business expands.

Investor Expectations and Control:

Equity-based financing options, such as venture capital or angel investments, may involve giving up partial ownership or control of your business.

Mitigation Strategies:

Conduct thorough due diligence on potential

investors and understand their expectations, goals, and involvement in your business. Negotiate terms and conditions that protect your interests and ensure alignment between your vision and the investor's objectives. Seek legal and financial advice to navigate complex equity financing agreements.

Regulatory and Compliance Risks:

Depending on the type of alternative financing there may be specific regulatory requirements and compliance obligations to meet.

Mitigation Strategies:

Familiarize yourself with applicable regulations and compliance obligations related to the chosen financing option. Seek professional guidance to ensure compliance with legal and regulatory frameworks. Maintain accurate financial records and documentation to facilitate audits and reporting.

Reputation and Public Perception:

Crowdfunding or peer to peer lending campaigns are publicly visible, and the success or failure of such initiatives can impact your brand reputation.

Mitigation Strategies:

Develop a clear communication strategy to effectively convey your business's purpose, goals, and financial needs to potential funders. Maintain transparency and accountability throughout the financing process.

Address any concerns or negative feedback promptly and professionally to safeguard your reputation.

Cash Flow Impact:

Some alternative financing methods, such as revenue-based financing or merchant cash advances, may involve regular deductions from your cash flow.

Mitigation Strategies:

Carefully analyze the impact of repayment terms on your cash flow and ensure it remains sustainable. Consider the potential fluctuations in revenue and evaluate whether the financing option aligns with your business's revenue cycles.

Reliance on External Factors:

Alternative financing options, such as grants or government funding, may depend on external factors beyond your control, such as eligibility criteria, competition, or available funding.

Mitigation Strategies:

Conduct thorough research and understand the requirements and limitations of the chosen alternative financing method. Determine alternative financing options that offer a diverse range of funding sources to reduce reliance on any single option. Develop backup plans or alternative funding strategies in case certain options are not feasible or available.

Limited Support and Resources:

Unlike traditional lenders, alternative financing providers may offer limited support and resources beyond the funding itself.

Mitigation Strategies:

Assess the level of support and resources provided by the financing provider and determine if it aligns with your business needs. Seek additional support from professional advisors, mentors, or industry networks to fill any gaps in expertise or guidance.

Complexity and Due Diligence:

Alternative financing options can be complex, requiring careful due diligence and legal considerations.

Mitigation Strategies:

Engage legal and financial professionals with expertise in alternative financing to guide you through the process. Conduct thorough due diligence on financing providers, investors, or crowdfunding platforms to ensure their legitimacy and track record. By understanding and addressing the potential risks associated with alternative financing, businesses can make informed decisions and implement appropriate mitigation strategies. It is crucial to assess the risks alongside the benefits of each financing option and evaluate their alignment with your business goals and financial needs. Seeking professional advice, conducting thorough research, and maintaining transparency throughout the process will contribute to a successful and well-managed alternative financing strategy.

Chapter 17

NAVIGATING THE FINANCING LANDSCAPE

In this final chapter, we will explore key considerations and practical tips for navigating the financing landscape and implementing effective strategies for business financing. Whether you choose traditional financing options, leverage tax incentives, establish a trust, or explore alternative financing methods, these guidelines will help you make informed decisions and optimize your financial position.

Comprehensive Financial Planning:

Develop a comprehensive financial plan that aligns with your business goals and outlines your short-term and long-term funding needs. Identify the specific purposes for financing, such as expansion, equipment purchase, or research and development, and estimate the required funding amounts. Regularly review and update your financial plan to accommodate changing business needs and evolving market conditions.

Diversify Funding Sources:

Explore multiple financing options and diversify your funding sources to reduce reliance on a single source. Consider a combination of traditional and alternative

financing methods to access capital from different channels. By diversifying, you can mitigate risks and increase your chances of securing the necessary funding.

Build Strong Relationships:

Cultivate relationships with financial institutions, lenders, investors, and other key stakeholders in the financing landscape. Attending networking events, industry conferences, and workshops to connect with potential funders and advisors. Strong relationships can enhance your credibility, increase access to funding opportunities,

and provide valuable guidance and support.

Seek Professional Advice:

Engage the services of experienced financial advisors, accountants, and legal professionals who specialize in business financing. They can provide valuable insights, help you navigate complex financial regulations, and ensure compliance with tax and legal requirements. Professional advice can significantly contribute to the success of your financing endeavors.

Thoroughly Research Financing Options:

Conduct thorough research on different financing options, including interest rates, repayment terms, eligibility criteria, and associated costs. Compare the pros and cons of each option and evaluate their suitability for your specific business needs and financial objectives. Consider the availability, scalability, and potential risks associated with each financing method.

Prepare Strong Applications:

When applying for financing, prepare strong and well-documented applications that clearly articulate your business's financial position, growth potential, and repayment capacity. Include comprehensive financial statements, cash flow projections, business plans, and any supporting documents required by the financing provider. A strong application increases your chances of securing funding and demonstrates your commitment to responsible financial management.

Monitor and Manage Cash Flow:

Implement robust cash flow management practices to ensure optimal utilization of funds and timely repayment of loans. Regularly monitor your cash flow, track expenses, and optimize revenue generation strategies. Effective cash flow management helps build a positive credit history, improves your financial position, and enhances your credibility with lenders.

Maintain Transparent Financial Records:

Keep accurate and up-to-date financial records, including income statements, balance sheets, tax returns, and supporting documents. Transparent financial records demonstrate your financial stability, facilitate loan applications, and simplify compliance with tax and regulatory obligations. Utilize financial management tools or software to streamline record-keeping processes and maintain organized financial documentation.

Stay Informed About Tax Incentives:

Regularly research and stay informed about tax incentives and credits available to businesses in your industry and region. Consult with tax professionals or advisors to identify potential tax incentives that can reduce your tax burden and improve your cash flow. Maximize the benefits of tax incentives by understanding the eligibility criteria, filing requirements, and deadlines.

Continuously Evaluate and Adapt:

Regularly evaluate the effectiveness of your financing strategies and make necessary adjustments based on changing business needs, market conditions, and financing landscape. Monitor the performance of your financing options, reassess their alignment with your business goals, and explore new opportunities as they arise. A proactive and adaptable approach to financing ensures that your business remains well-positioned for growth and success. By incorporating these guidelines into your financing approach, you can navigate the complex landscape of business financing with confidence and maximize your chances of securing the necessary funding. Remember to continuously educate yourself on industry trends, seek professional advice when needed, and adapt your strategies to the evolving financial landscape. With careful planning, research, and execution, you can build a strong financial foundation for your business and fuel its growth and success.

Chapter 18

NAVIGATING THE FINANCING PROCESS

In this chapter, we will delve into the practical steps involved in navigating the financing process for your business. From preparing your financial documents to negotiating terms and closing the deal, understanding the key stages and best practices will help you navigate the process successfully.

Assessing Your Financing Needs:

Begin by assessing your business's financing needs and determining the specific purpose for seeking funding. Evaluate the amount of capital required and the timeframe for accessing the funds. Consider your business's growth plans, operational expenses, and any upcoming investment opportunities.

Creating a Comprehensive Financial Plan:

Develop a comprehensive financial plan that outlines your projected revenue, expenses, and cash flow. Include financial projections for the next few years, highlighting key milestones and growth targets. Your financial plan will serve as a roadmap for understanding your funding requirements and presenting a clear picture to potential lenders or investors.

Gathering Financial Documents:

Prepare all the necessary financial documents to support your funding application. This may include business tax returns, income statements, balance sheets, bank statements, and cash flow projections. Ensure that your financial documents are accurate, up-to-date, and reflect the financial health and stability of your business.

Researching Financing Options:

Conduct thorough research to identify financing

options that align with your business needs. Explore traditional lenders, alternative financing methods, government programs, venture capital firms, angel investors, or crowdfunding platforms. Evaluate the eligibility criteria, terms, interest rates, and repayment options of each financing option.

Building Relationships:

Cultivate relationships with potential lenders, investors, and financing institutions. Attend networking events, industry conferences, and pitch competitions to connect with key stakeholders in the financing landscape. Building strong relationships can increase your chances of securing funding and provide valuable guidance and support throughout the process.

Preparing a Strong Funding Proposal:

Craft a compelling funding proposal that clearly communicates your business concept, market opportunity, competitive advantage, and growth potential. Include a detailed description of your funding needs, the purpose of the funds, and how the funds will be utilized to drive business growth. Highlight the financial viability and potential returns for potential lenders or investors.

Applying for Financing:

Once you have identified the most suitable financing option, follow the application process outlined by the financing provider. Prepare your application package, including your funding proposal, financial documents, business plan, and any additional supporting materials required. Ensure that your application is complete, accurate, and submitted within the specified deadlines.

Negotiating Terms and Conditions:

If your application is successful, you may enter negotiations with the financing provider to determine the terms and conditions of the funding. Review the proposed terms and evaluate their impact on your business. Negotiate favorable terms, including interest rates, repayment schedules, collateral requirements, and any other relevant conditions.

Conducting Due Diligence:

During the financing process, the financing provider may conduct due diligence to assess the viability of your business and the risks involved. Be prepared to provide additional documentation or answer inquiries related to your business operations, financials, and growth plans. Cooperate fully and promptly to demonstrate transparency and build trust with the financing provider.

Closing the Deal:

Once the negotiations are finalized, and all due diligence has been completed, you will proceed to the closing stage. Review the final terms and conditions, ensuring that they align with the agreed-upon terms. Sign the necessary agreements, obtain legal advice if required, and fulfill any remaining requirements to close the deal.

Managing and Repaying the Financing:

Once you have secured the funding, carefully manage the funds, and use them according to the agreed-upon purpose. Develop a repayment plan and ensure timely repayments to maintain a positive relationship with the financing provider. Regularly review your financials and adjust your repayment strategy as needed. Building and Maintaining Strong Relationships: Foster strong relationships with your financing providers, keeping them updated on your business's progress and milestones.

Maintain open lines of communication, provide regular financial reports, and address any concerns promptly. A positive relationship can lead to future funding opportunities and continued support for your business.

Navigating the financing process requires careful planning, preparation, and engagement with potential lenders or investors. By following these steps and best practices, you can streamline the financing process and increase your chances of securing the necessary funding to fuel your

business's growth and success. Remember to stay organized, communicate effectively, and remain flexible throughout the process.

Chapter 19

CASE STUDIES: SUCCESSFUL BUSINESS FINANCING STRATEGIES

In this chapter, we will explore real-life case studies of successful business financing strategies implemented by companies across different industries. By examining these examples, you can gain valuable insights into the practical application of various financing methods and the factors that contributed to their success.

Case Study 1:

XYZ Tech - Venture Capital Funding XYZ Tech, a technology startup specializing in artificial intelligence, successfully secured venture capital funding to fuel its expansion and product development. The company's financing strategy involved the following key elements:

1. Compelling Business Plan: XYZ Tech developed a comprehensive business plan that highlighted the market potential, competitive advantage, and revenue projections. The plan effectively communicated the company's growth trajectory and the value proposition to potential investors.

2. Product Development Milestones: The company demonstrated a clear roadmap for product development, showcasing key milestones and the anticipated impact on market share and revenue growth. This provided investors with confidence in the company's ability to execute its strategy.

3. Strong Team and Advisory Board: XYZ Tech assembled a team of experienced professionals with a proven track record in the technology industry. The company also formed an advisory board comprising industry experts, which added

credibility and guidance to its operations.

4. Market Validation: XYZ Tech conducted thorough market research and validation, demonstrating a demand for its AI technology solutions. The company secured pilot projects and early customers, providing evidence of market traction and potential revenue streams.

5. Effective Pitching and Relationship Building: The company's management team actively participated in pitch competitions, industry events, and networking opportunities to connect with venture capital firms. They refined their pitching skills and built relationships with potential investors, cultivating trust and rapport.

Case Study 2:

ABC Manufacturing - Bank Loan and Government Grants

ABC Manufacturing, a medium-sized manufacturing company, successfully accessed funding through a combination of bank loans and government grants. The company's financing strategy included the following key elements:

Solid Financials and Track Record: ABC Manufacturing maintained strong financial statements, demonstrating consistent profitability, cash flow management, and a healthy balance sheet. The company's track record of success and financial stability positioned it as a low-risk borrower.

Strategic Growth Plan: The company developed a strategic growth plan that outlined its expansion initiatives, including new product lines, market expansion, and facility upgrades. The plan provided a clear vision of the company's future and the funding required to achieve its objectives.

Bank Relationship and Collateral: ABC Manufacturing maintained a long-standing relationship with a local bank. The company worked closely with the bank to present a comprehensive loan proposal supported by collateral, such as machinery and property assets. The existing relationship and collateral strengthened the loan application.

Government Grants and Incentives: ABC Manufacturing conducted thorough research to identify government grants and incentives applicable to its industry. The company successfully secured grants for research and development projects, innovation, and workforce training, further reducing its financial burden.

Proactive Compliance and Reporting: The company ensured compliance with loan covenants, government grant requirements, and reporting obligations. ABC Manufacturing maintained open lines of communication with the bank and government agencies, providing timely updates and documentation.

Case Study 3:

DEF Retail - Crowdfunding Campaign DEF Retail, a boutique retail store specializing in sustainable fashion, successfully raised funds through a crowdfunding campaign to support its store expansion. The company's financing strategy incorporated the following key elements:

1. Compelling Brand Story: DEF Retail crafted a compelling brand story that highlighted its commitment to sustainability, ethical practices, and unique fashion offerings. The company effectively communicated its mission and values to resonate with potential backers.

2. Engaging Crowdfunding Platform: DEF Retail selected a reputable crowdfunding platform known for its focus on sustainable businesses and aligned values. The company utilized the platform's built-in marketing tools and resources to reach a broader audience and

attract backers.

3. Rewards-based Incentives: DEF Retail offered attractive rewards-based incentives to incentivize backers to contribute to the crowdfunding campaign. These incentives ranged from exclusive merchandise, discounts, and personalized shopping experiences, creating a sense of exclusivity and value for supporters.

4. social media and Influencer Marketing: The company leveraged social media platforms and collaborated with influencers and brand ambassadors to raise awareness about its crowdfunding campaign. By tapping into their existing networks and engaged followers, DEF Retail expanded its reach and generated momentum for the campaign.

Transparent Communication and Updates: DEF Retail maintained transparent communication with its backers throughout the campaign. Regular updates, progress reports, and behind-the-scenes content were shared to keep supporters engaged and informed about the campaign's status.

6. Community Engagement: The company actively engaged with its community of customers, fashion enthusiasts, and sustainability advocates. DEF Retail organized events, workshops, and collaborations that further promoted its brand and crowdfunding efforts, fostering a sense of community and support.

By examining these case studies, you can draw inspiration and key takeaways for your own business financing strategies. Keep in mind that each business is unique, and the success of a financing strategy depends on various factors, including industry dynamics, market conditions, and the specific goals of your business. Adapt and tailor these strategies to suit your business's needs and leverage the lessons learned from successful cases to enhance your financing approach.

… Chapter 20

SECURING FUNDING THROUGH EQUITY FINANCING

Equity financing is a form of business financing where companies raise funds by selling ownership shares, or equity, in the business. In this chapter, we will delve into the details of securing funding through equity financing and explore the benefits, considerations, and strategies associated with this financing option.

1. Benefits of Equity Financing:

Access to Capital: Equity financing allows businesses to raise significant capital to support their growth initiatives, such as expanding operations, developing new products, or entering new markets. Shared Risk: By bringing in equity investors, businesses can share the financial risk and burden with external parties, reducing the potential strain on the company's resources. Expertise and Network: Equity investors often bring valuable expertise, industry connections, and mentorship to the table, which can enhance the business's strategic direction and accelerate growth. Potential for Exponential Returns: If the business performs well, equity investors stand to benefit from the company's success through capital appreciation and potential dividends.

2. Types of Equity Financing:

Angel Investors: Individual investors who provide capital in exchange for equity. They typically invest in early-stage businesses and offer mentorship and guidance.

Venture Capital: Institutional investors who invest larger amounts of capital in high-growth potential companies. They often provide not only funding but also strategic support and industry expertise.

Private Equity: Investment firms that invest in

established companies seeking growth or restructuring. Private equity firms usually acquire a significant stake in the company and actively participate in its management. Initial Public Offering (IPO): The process of offering shares to the public for the first time through a stock exchange. This allows the company to raise substantial capital from public investors.

3. Considerations for Equity Financing:

Dilution of Ownership: When selling equity, the business owner relinquishes a portion of ownership and control over the company. It's essential to evaluate the trade-off between capital infusion and retaining ownership.

Investor Alignment: Choose equity investors who align with the company's vision, values, and long-term goals. Look for investors who bring strategic value beyond capital, such as industry experience, networks, and mentorship. Valuation and Terms: Determine a fair valuation for your business based on its financial performance, market potential, and comparable industry transactions. Negotiate favorable terms, including share price, governance rights, and exit strategies.

Legal and Regulatory Compliance: Equity financing involves legal and regulatory considerations. Seek professional advice to ensure compliance with securities laws, disclosure requirements, and investor protections.

4. Strategies for Securing Equity Financing:

Prepare a Comprehensive Business Plan: Create a detailed business plan that articulates your company's growth potential, market positioning, and competitive advantage. Highlight the market opportunity and the scalability of your business model. Build a Strong Management Team: Investors are often attracted to businesses with a capable and experienced management team. Surround yourself with skilled professionals who can drive the company's growth and execution.

Network and Pitch to Investors: Attend industry events, networking sessions, and pitch competitions to connect with potential equity investors. Craft a compelling and persuasive pitch that clearly communicates the business's value proposition and growth potential.

Engage with Angel Investor Groups and Venture Capital Firms: Research and reach out to angel investor groups and venture capital firms that specialize in your industry or business stage. Understand their investment criteria and tailor your approach accordingly.

Leverage Online Equity Crowdfunding Platforms: Explore online equity crowdfunding platforms that connect businesses with a broader pool of potential investors. These platforms allow businesses to raise funds from a larger network of individual investors.

5. Due Diligence and Documentation:

Equity financing involves thorough due diligence by investors. Be prepared to provide comprehensive financial statements, business projections, market analysis, and legal documentation. Engage legal and financial professionals to

review and prepare the necessary legal agreements, such as shareholders' agreements, subscription agreements, and term sheets. Remember that equity financing is a significant decision that impacts the ownership structure and future of your business. Carefully evaluate the pros and cons, align your financing strategy with your long-term goals, and seek professional guidance to ensure a successful equity financing process.

Chapter 21

Funding Strategies for Startups and Small Businesses

Startups and small businesses often face unique challenges when it comes to securing funding. In this chapter, we will explore funding strategies tailored specifically for startups and small businesses, considering their specific needs and limitations. These strategies can help entrepreneurs navigate the funding landscape and increase their chances of obtaining the necessary capital to fuel their growth.

1. Bootstrapping:

Bootstrapping involves funding the business with personal savings, revenue generated by business, or support from friends and family. This strategy allows entrepreneurs to maintain full control over their business but may limit the speed of growth. Bootstrapping requires a focus on lean operations, prioritizing essential expenses, and maximizing revenue generation to fund ongoing operations and growth.

2. Friends and Family:

Turning to friends and family for financial support can be an accessible funding option for startups and small businesses. However, it's essential to approach these arrangements professionally and with clear expectations.

Create formal agreements, outline repayment terms, and consider potential impacts on personal relationships. Maintain open communication to manage expectations and ensure transparency.

3. Crowdfunding:

Crowdfunding platforms provide a way to raise funds from a large pool of individuals who believe in your business idea or product. It involves presenting your business or project on a crowdfunding platform and seeking contributions from backers in exchange for rewards or equity. Rewards-based crowdfunding platforms like Kickstarter and Indiegogo allow entrepreneurs to pre-sell products or offer unique experiences to backers.

Equity crowdfunding platforms enable startups to sell shares of their company to a broader pool of investors.

4. Small Business Grants and Competitions:

Explore opportunities for small business grants and competitions, which provide non-repayable funds or in-kind support for startups and small businesses. Research government grants, industry-specific grants, and private organizations that offer financial assistance. Additionally, participate in business plan competitions and pitch events that offer cash prizes and exposure.

5. Microloans and Community Development

Financial Institutions (CDFIs):

Microloans are small loans typically offered by community-based organizations and CDFIs. They provide funding to startups and small businesses that may not qualify for traditional bank loans. These loans often have more flexible eligibility criteria and may come with mentorship or business support services to help entrepreneurs succeed.

6. Angel Investors:

Angel investors are high-net-worth individuals who provide capital and expertise to early-stage businesses in exchange for equity. They often invest in industries they have experience in and can provide valuable mentorship and industry connections. Network within the startup and entrepreneurial community to identify angel investors who align with your business goals and can contribute beyond just funding.

7. Venture Capital:

Venture capital firms invest in high-growth startups with the potential for significant returns. They typically provide larger amounts of funding and actively participate in the company's strategic direction. Prepare a comprehensive business plan, pitch deck, and financial projections to attract venture capital investors. Build relationships with venture capital firms and leverage your network for introductions.

8. Incubators and Accelerators:

Joining an incubator or accelerator program can provide startups with not only funding but also access to mentorship, resources, and a supportive entrepreneurial community. Incubators offer a nurturing environment for early-stage startups, while accelerators focus on fast-tracking growth and preparing startups for funding opportunities.

9. Small Business Administration (SBA) Loans:

The U.S. Small Business Administration offers loan programs that provide financial support to small businesses. These loans are partially guaranteed by the SBA, reducing the risk for lenders, and improving the chances of approval. Explore SBA loan programs, such as the 7(a) Loan Program and the Microloan Program, which offer flexible terms and competitive interest rates.

10. Strategic Partnerships and Corporate Sponsorships:

Seek out strategic partnerships and corporate sponsorships with larger companies in your industry. These partnerships can provide financial support, access to resources, distribution channels, and market validation. Remember that funding strategies for startups and small businesses often require a combination of different approaches. Assess your specific funding needs, align them with the available options, and develop a comprehensive funding strategy that suits your business's unique requirements. Be proactive in building relationships, leveraging your network, and continuously refining your pitch and business plan to increase your chances of securing the funding you need.

Conclusion:

Unlocking the Power of Business Financing

Congratulations! You've reached the end of this comprehensive guide on strategies for business financing, tax incentives, and the benefits of having a trust. Throughout this book, we have explored various aspects of business financing, delving into traditional and alternative funding options, tax incentives, trust structures, and effective financial management techniques. We began by emphasizing the importance of understanding business financing and the key factors to consider when evaluating funding options. We discussed the significance of financial planning, risk assessment, and the alignment of financing strategies with long-term business goals. By establishing a solid foundation of financial knowledge, you are better equipped to make informed decisions and navigate the complex world of business financing. We then explored the potential tax incentives available to businesses, highlighting their significance in reducing tax liabilities and increasing cash flow. By leveraging tax incentives effectively, businesses can optimize their financial position and allocate resources to growth initiatives. Understanding the tax landscape and working closely with tax professionals can help you uncover opportunities for tax savings and compliance. In addition to tax incentives, we explored the benefits of establishing a trust structure for business financing. Trusts offer asset protection, privacy, and estate planning advantages that can contribute to the long-term stability and growth of your business. We discussed the different types of trusts and their specific benefits, emphasizing the importance of seeking professional advice to establish and manage trusts effectively.

Furthermore, we delved into the various strategies for securing funding, including traditional options like bank loans and lines of credit, as well as alternative approaches such as crowdfunding, angel investments, and venture capital. Each financing avenue comes with its own considerations and requirements, and we provided guidance on how to navigate the financing process and optimize your chances of securing the funding you need.

To ensure the longevity and success of your business, we also discussed the importance of managing and optimizing your finances. We explored strategies for cash flow management, budgeting, financial analysis, cost optimization, financial controls, and reporting. By adopting these practices, you can maintain financial stability, make informed decisions, and position your business for sustainable growth.

Lastly, we examined case studies of successful business financing strategies, highlighting real-world examples of how businesses effectively utilized various financing options to achieve their objectives. These case studies provided valuable insights and inspiration for implementing similar strategies in your own business.

Remember, business financing is not a one size fits all approach. Each business is unique, and it is crucial to assess your specific needs, goals, and circumstances when formulating your financing strategies. Seek professional advice, conduct thorough research, and continuously evaluate and adjust your financial plans to adapt to market conditions and seize new opportunities.

By leveraging the knowledge and strategies presented in this book, you are well-equipped to make informed financial decisions, maximize your funding potential, and ultimately drive the growth and success of your business. As you embark on your business financing journey, always remain open to learning, embrace innovation, and never hesitate to seek the expertise and guidance of professionals.

Wishing you great success in your business endeavors and a prosperous future fueled by strategic and effective financing!

www.ingramcontent.com/pod-product-compliance
Lightning Source LLC
Chambersburg PA
CBHW030622220526
45463CB00004B/1384